THE
PLEASURES
OF GOD
DVD STUDY GUIDE

JOHN PIPER

THE
PLEASURES
OF GOD
DVD STUDY GUIDE

Meditations on God's Delight in Being God

MULTNOMAH
BOOKS

THE PLEASURES OF GOD DVD STUDY GUIDE
PUBLISHED BY MULTNOMAH BOOKS
12265 Oracle Boulevard, Suite 200
Colorado Springs, Colorado 80921

ISBN 978-1-60142-290-3
ISBN 978-1-60142-293-4 (electronic)

Cover design by Kristopher Orr; cover photograph © John Cancalosi, Getty Images

Published in the United States by WaterBrook Multnomah, an imprint of the Crown Publishing Group, a division of Random House Inc., New York.

MULTNOMAH and its mountain colophon are registered trademarks of Random House Inc.

Printed in the United States of America
2012—First Edition

10 9 8 7 6 5 4 3 2 1

SPECIAL SALES

Most WaterBrook Multnomah books are available at special quantity discounts when purchased in bulk by corporations, organizations, and special-interest groups. Custom imprinting or excerpting can also be done to fit special needs. For information, please e-mail SpecialMarkets@WaterBrookMultnomah.com or call 1-800-603-7051.

Note: Page references in the book *The Pleasures of God* cited in this study guide correspond to the paperback edition published in 2012.

CONTENTS

    God's Pleasure in Bruising His Son 113

LESSON 12
    Review and Conclusion 125

    Leaders Guide 127

    Appendix A: Six-Session Intensive Option 132

    Appendix B: Leading Productive Discussions 133

    Notes 136

INTRODUCTION
TO THIS STUDY GUIDE

The world is filled with admiration. People are constantly admiring celebrities, politicians, athletes, lovers, friends, relatives, and natural wonders. Rarely in this sea of admiration do we find people enthralled with that which is truly captivating. Instead, individuals spend their time chasing the latest fad, hoping to derive some small satisfaction from enjoying the rotten crumbs of this world. And the world seems increasingly unable to determine what things are truly worthy of admiration and reflection. Paul's exhortation to the church at Philippi is rarely heeded: "Finally, brothers, whatever is true, whatever is honorable, whatever is just, whatever is pure, whatever is lovely, whatever is commendable, if there is any excellence, if there is anything worthy of praise, think about these things" (Philippians 4:8).

In the introduction to the book *The Pleasures of God,* John Piper exposes the crying need of the hour: "What the church and the world need today, more than anything else, is to know and love God—the great, glorious, sovereign, happy God of the Bible. Very few people think of God as supremely happy in the fellowship of the Trinity and in the work of creation and redemption. The volcanic exuberance of God over the worth of his Son and the work of his hands and the welfare of his people is not well-known. God's delight in being God is not sung the way it should be, with wonder and passion, in the worship places of the world. And we are the poorer and weaker for it."[1]

The aim of this study guide is to consider the worth and excellency of God through the lens of his happiness. The central question that we will address is this: "What are the things that bring the greatest joy and delight to God?" In answering this question, our hope is that thousands would be awakened to the excellency and glory of the supremely happy God, who is worthy of all of our worship and admiration. In unfolding God's delight in being God, we hope that many will become increasingly satisfied in God and more fully transformed into his likeness, all to the praise of his glory.

This study guide is designed to be used in a twelve-session[2] guided group study that focuses on *The Pleasures of God* DVD set.[3] After an introductory lesson, each subsequent lesson examines one thirty-minute session[4] from *The Pleasures of God* DVD set. You, the learner, are encouraged to prepare for the viewing of each session by reading and reflecting upon Scripture, by considering key quotations, and by asking yourself penetrating questions. Your preparatory work for each lesson is marked with the heading "Before You Watch the DVD, Study and Prepare" in Lessons 2–11.

The workload is conveniently divided into five daily, manageable assignments. There is also a section suggesting further study. This work is to be completed individually before the group convenes to view the DVD and discuss the material.

Throughout this study guide, paragraphs printed in this typeface are excerpts from a book written by John Piper or excerpts from the Desiring God website. They are included to supplement the study questions and to summarize key or provocative points.

The second section in Lessons 2–11, titled "Further Up and Further In," is designed for the learner who wants to explore the concepts and ideas introduced in the lesson in greater detail. This section is not required, but it will deepen your understanding of the material. This section requires that you read online sermons or articles from the Desiring God website (www.desiringgod.org) and answer relevant questions. These sermons can be found by performing a title search at the Desiring God website.

The third section in Lessons 2–11, titled "While You Watch the DVD, Take Notes," is to be completed while the DVD is playing. This section includes fill-in-the-blanks and leaves space for note taking. You are encouraged to engage with the DVD by filling in the appropriate blanks and writing down other notes that will aid you in the group discussion.

The fourth section in each normal lesson is "After You Watch the DVD, Discuss What You've Learned." Three discussion questions are provided to guide and focus the conversation. You may record, in the spaces provided, notes that will help you contribute to the conversation. Or you may use this space to record things from the discussion that you want to remember.

The fifth and final section is an application section: "After You Discuss, Make Application." You will be challenged to record a takeaway point and to engage in a certain activity that is a fitting response to the content presented in the lesson.

Group leaders will want to peruse the Leaders Guide, which is included at the end of this study guide.

Life transformation will only occur by the grace of God. Therefore, we highly encourage you to seek the Lord in prayer throughout the learning process. Pray that God would open your eyes to see wonderful things in his Word. Pray that he would grant you the insight and concentration you need in order to get the most from this resource. Pray that God would cause you not merely to understand the truth but also to rejoice in it. And pray that the discussion in your group would be mutually encouraging and edifying. We've included objectives at the beginning of each lesson. These objectives won't be realized without the gracious work of God through prayer.

INTRODUCTION TO *THE PLEASURES OF GOD*

LESSON OBJECTIVES

It is our prayer that after you have finished this lesson...

- You will have a better sense of how you and others view God's emotional life.
- Your curiosity will be roused, and questions will come to mind.
- You will be eager to explore what things God delights in.

ABOUT YOURSELF

1. What is your name?
2. Tell the group members something about yourself that they probably don't already know.
3. What are you hoping to learn from this study?

A PREVIEW OF *THE PLEASURES OF GOD*

1. When you think about God, what emotions come to mind? Do you think God is primarily happy? sad? frustrated? rejoicing? angry? Explain your answer.

2. What comes into your mind when you think about the
   pleasures of God? Make a list of things that you think God
   takes pleasure and delight in. What do you think God delights
   in above all else?

THE WORTH AND EXCELLENCY OF GOD'S SOUL

A Companion Study to The Pleasures of God *DVD, Session 1*

LESSON OBJECTIVES

It is our prayer that after you have finished this lesson…
- You will reflect on what makes a soul worthy and excellent.
- You will begin to ask what brings God pleasure.
- You will grow in your desire to find your satisfaction in God.

—•» *Before You Watch the DVD, Study and Prepare* «•—

DAY 1—THE EXCELLENCY OF THE SOUL

As we begin this study, we invite you to reflect upon someone whom you admire and respect.

* **Question 1:** Why do you admire this person? What makes him or her admirable? How do we assess a person's worthiness and excellence? Is a person excellent because of his thoughts? his desires? his actions? something else? Record your reflections in the space below.[5]

Question 2: What makes God excellent? What should we admire about God?

DAY 2—THE THIRST OF A SOUL

Many times in the Bible we come across verses that describe a person or a soul as thirsting or hungering after something that will bring satisfaction. "Like cold water to a *thirsty* soul, so is good news from a far country" (Proverbs 25:25). "Come, everyone who *thirsts,* come to the waters; and he who has no money, come, buy and eat!" (Isaiah 55:1). "Blessed are those who *hunger and thirst* for righteousness" (Matthew 5:6). What is the deepest thirst or longing of the human soul?

Study Psalm 63:1–4.

[1]O God, you are my God; earnestly I seek you; my soul thirsts for you; my flesh faints for you, as in a dry and weary land where there is no water. [2]So I have looked upon you in the sanctuary, beholding your power and glory. [3]Because your steadfast love is better than life, my lips will praise you. [4]So I will bless you as long as I live; in your name I will lift up my hands.

Question 3: According to these verses, what is David's deepest desire? Why does he desire this?

* **Question 4:** John Piper explains that in Psalm 63 David does not primarily thirst after God's gifts but after God *himself.* "It is a thirst for God. David has a heart for God. He has a taste for fellowship with God."[6] Would you say that you personally have a "taste for fellowship with God"? Do you believe that God is able to give you this sort of renewed "taste" for him?

Day 3—The Power of a Sentence

Consider the following quotation from John Piper's message "Quantitative Hopelessness and the Immeasurable Moment" on the life-changing power of sentences:

> What I have learned from about twenty years of serious reading is this. It is sentences that change my life, not books. What changes my life is some new glimpse of truth, some powerful challenge, some resolution to a long-standing dilemma, and these usually come concentrated in a sentence or two. I do not remember 99% of what I read, but if the 1% of each book or article I do remember is a life-changing insight, then I don't begrudge the 99%. And that life-changing insight usually comes in a moment, a moment whose value is all out of proportion to its little size. That's why I call it an "immeasurable moment."

Question 5: Think of a time in your life when you were significantly affected by a sentence that you read. What was that
sentence? How did it impact you?

In 1986, John Piper read a single sentence written by Henry Scougal
that prompted him to preach a series of sermons and write a book on "the
pleasures of God." Scougal wrote this in his book *The Life of God in the
Soul of Man:*

The worth and excellency of the soul is to be measured
by the object of its love.[7]

* **Question 6:** Rewrite this quotation in your own words. Do you
agree with Scougal?

DAY 4—DOES *GOD* HAVE A SOUL?

* **Question 7:** When Henry Scougal wrote, "The worth and excellency of the soul is to be measured by the object of its love," he
was speaking of *human* souls. Do you think that the same
principle could be applied to measure the excellency and worth
of *God's* "soul"? Why or why not?

There are several passages in Scripture that speak of God doing
something from his heart or soul, as in Jeremiah 32:41.

Study Jeremiah 32:36–41.

[36]Now therefore thus says the LORD, the God of Israel, concerning this city of which you say, "It is given into the hand of the king of Babylon by sword, by famine, and by pestilence": [37]Behold, I will gather them from all the countries to which I drove them in my anger and my wrath and in great indignation. I will bring them back to this place, and I will make them dwell in safety. [38]And they shall be my people, and I will be their God. [39]I will give them one heart and one way, that they may fear me forever, for their own good and the good of their children after them. [40]I will make with them an everlasting covenant, that I will not turn away from doing good to them. And I will put the fear of me in their hearts, that they may not turn from me. [41]I will rejoice in doing them good, and I will plant them in this land in faithfulness, with all my heart and all my soul.

Question 8: What do these verses tell us about God's "soul" and what brings him joy?

DAY 5—SATISFY US, LORD!

In the Psalms we are often confronted by expressions of both intense pain and pleasure, very often in the same psalm. These writers felt deeply about God, with both feet in the real world marked by sin and suffering. Moses, the writer of Psalm 90, and believers throughout the ages have prayed, "Return, O LORD! How long?" in the face of life's brevity and difficulty while also praying, "Satisfy us…with your steadfast love," trusting in the joy-giving goodness of God.

Study Psalm 90:9–17.

⁹For all our days pass away under your wrath; we bring our years to an end like a sigh. ¹⁰The years of our life are seventy, or even by reason of strength eighty; yet their span is but toil and trouble; they are soon gone, and we fly away. ¹¹Who considers the power of your anger, and your wrath according to the fear of you? ¹²So teach us to number our days that we may get a heart of wisdom. ¹³Return, O LORD! How long? Have pity on your servants! ¹⁴Satisfy us in the morning with your steadfast love, that we may rejoice and be glad all our days. ¹⁵Make us glad for as many days as you have afflicted us, and for as many years as we have seen evil. ¹⁶Let your work be shown to your servants, and your glorious power to their children. ¹⁷Let the favor of the Lord our God be upon us, and establish the work of our hands upon us; yes, establish the work of our hands!

Question 9: What do these verses teach us about the shortness and difficulty of life in this fallen world?

* Question 10: What things in life often "satisfy us" and "make us glad"? What does Moses in this psalm want to be satisfied with and gladdened by? What personal response is God calling us to make to this portion of his Word?

FURTHER UP AND FURTHER IN

Note: The "Further Up and Further In" section is for those who want to study more. It is a section for further reference and going deeper. The phrase "further up and further in" is borrowed from C. S. Lewis.

As noted in the introduction, each lesson in this study guide provides the opportunity for you to do further study. In this section, you will have the opportunity to read a sermon or article and answer some questions about what you have read.

Read "The Life of God in the Soul of Man," an online sermon at the Desiring God website.

> **Question 11:** What is the central truth that Henry Scougal and John Piper make about "true religion"?

> **Question 12:** Describe three results of the life of God in the soul of man.

> **Question 13:** According to this sermon, why might God be considered schizophrenic? How does Paul address this misconception? Describe the harmony that John Piper sees in the Trinitarian work of redemption.

Study Romans 8:9–11.

⁹You, however, are not in the flesh but in the Spirit, if in fact the Spirit of God dwells in you. Anyone who does not have the Spirit of Christ does not belong to him. ¹⁰But if Christ is in you, although the body is dead because of sin, the Spirit is life because of righteousness. ¹¹If the Spirit of him who raised Jesus from the dead dwells in you, he who raised Christ Jesus from the dead will also give life to your mortal bodies through his Spirit who dwells in you.

Question 14: What different ways is the Spirit referred to in this passage? How might this give us insight into the unified work of the Father, Son, and Spirit in redemption? What do you think Paul means when he says that the Spirit "dwells in you" (three times in these verses)?

Read "Christian, Know Whose You Are," an online sermon at the Desiring God website.

Question 15: What are at least five things that make believers different from unbelievers?

—→ *While You Watch the DVD, Take Notes* ←—

In Psalm 90:14, the psalmist is saying to God, "I'm not, and I _____ to be, and you're my only _____ that I _____ be."

Who was Henry Scougal? How did his life and writing influence Piper's *The Pleasures of God*?

What is one reason from Isaiah 57:1–2 that the righteous may have their lives cut short at an early age (like Henry Scougal did)?

Henry Scougal wrote: "The worth and excellency of a _____ is to be measured by the _____ of its _____."

John Piper concludes by saying that when love is _____ - _____ (that is, love has the right _____), the soul's *pleasures* are unsurpassed.

→❧ *After You Watch the DVD, Discuss What You've Learned* ❧←

1. Discuss John Piper's explanation of Psalm 90:14, which he paraphrases as "I'm not, and I need to be, and you're my only hope that I could be." Do you think that God is able and willing to satisfy your soul?

2. Do you agree with John Piper when he says, "With his unusual blessing we can do more in five minutes than we can in five years without him." Have you experienced God's unusual blessing at some time in your life?

3. When Henry Scougal wrote that "the worth and excellency of
    a soul is to be measured by the object of its love," what did he
    mean by the word *love*? Do you agree with this understanding
    of love?

—➤ *After You Discuss, Make Application* ✦—

1. What was the most meaningful part of this lesson for you?
    Was there a sentence, concept, or idea that really struck you?
    Why? Record your thoughts in the space below.

2. Compose a short prayer for yourself based on what you have
    learned in this lesson. Incorporate insights from Psalm 90:14
    and Scougal's sentence about the worth of a soul. Pray this
    prayer each day before you use this study guide.

OUR PLEASURE IN GOD'S WELL-PLACED PLEASURES

A Companion Study to The Pleasures of God *DVD, Session 2*

LESSON OBJECTIVES

It is our prayer that after you have finished this lesson…
- You will understand the importance of studying God's delights.
- You will see that the Christian's two great desires—to be happy and to glorify God—come together in our study of God's delights.
- Your vision of God will be expanded, and you will begin to be transformed into his image.

—❖ *Before You Watch the DVD, Study and Prepare* ❖—

DAY 1—WHAT MAKES EVIL EVIL?

What makes an action truly evil? Does evilness have to do mainly with harming other people? With breaking laws? With failing to live up to ideals of goodness? In answering these important questions, we should turn to examine God's Word.

Study Jeremiah 2:12–13.

¹²Be appalled, O heavens, at this; be shocked, be utterly desolate, declares the LORD, ¹³for my people have committed two evils: they have forsaken me, the fountain of living waters, and hewed out cisterns for themselves, broken cisterns that can hold no water.

* **Question 1:** What are the two evils that God's people had committed? How are these two evils related?

In this passage, "People are condemned for forsaking God and seeking their happiness elsewhere."[8] With this in mind, meditate on Jesus' words in John 5:39–40.

³⁹You search the Scriptures because you think that in them you have eternal life; and it is they that bear witness about me, ⁴⁰yet you refuse to come to me that you may have life.

Question 2: According to this passage, what is the fundamental problem of unbelief?

DAY 2—THE JOY OF YOUR MASTER

As noted in the introduction, this study will unfold a vision of God through the lens of his happiness. But why should we explore the worth of God's soul in this way? The first reason has to do with our hunger for happiness.

Many of us eagerly hope for the day when God himself will welcome us into the kingdom with the words "Well done, good and faithful servant" (Matthew 25:21). But how many of us reflect upon the rest of this verse?

Study Matthew 25:19–21.

> [19]Now after a long time the master of those servants came and settled accounts with them. [20]And he who had received the five talents came forward, bringing five talents more, saying, "Master, you delivered to me five talents; here I have made five talents more." [21]His master said to him, "Well done, good and faithful servant. You have been faithful over a little; I will set you over much. Enter into the joy of your master."

> *** Question 3:** According to this passage, what is the reward for our faithfulness? Why is the happiness of God so important in making this promise good news?

The promise of Matthew 25:21 invites us to consider the joy of our Master. Look now at the final verses of Jesus' high priestly prayer.

Read John 17:24–26.

> [24]Father, I desire that they also, whom you have given me, may be with me where I am, to see my glory that you have given me because you loved me before the foundation of the world. [25]O righteous Father, even though the world does not know you, I know you, and these know that you have sent me. [26]I made known to them your name, and I will continue to make it known, that the love with which you have loved me may be in them, and I in them.

Question 4: What two things does Jesus desire in verse 24? Why does Jesus make known the name of the Father to us? What implication does this have for our present study?

Imagine being able to enjoy what is most enjoyable with unbounded energy and passion forever. This is not now our experience.... But if the aim of Jesus in John 17:26 comes true, all this will change. If God's pleasure in the Son becomes our pleasure, then the object of our pleasure, Jesus, will be inexhaustible in personal worth. He will never become boring or disappointing or frustrating. No greater treasure can be conceived than the Son of God. Moreover, our ability to savor this inexhaustible treasure will not be limited by human weaknesses. We will enjoy the Son of God with the very enjoyment of his Father. God's delight in his Son will be in us and it will be ours.[9]

DAY 3—ALL TO GOD'S GLORY

What does our study of the pleasures of God have to do with the nitty-gritty details of our lives? What do the seemingly mundane decisions and actions of our lives reveal about the pleasures of our souls?

Consider 1 Corinthians 10:31 and Colossians 3:17.

> [31]So, whether you eat or drink, or whatever you do, do all to the glory of God. (1 Corinthians 10:31)

¹⁷And whatever you do, in word or deed, do everything in the name of the Lord Jesus, giving thanks to God the Father through him. (Colossians 3:17)

Question 5: How do you think someone can eat or drink to God's glory (1 Corinthians 10:31)? How does Paul's teaching in Colossians 3:17 help you answer this question?

* **Question 6:** Why do you think that God cares about how we go about the ordinary affairs of life, like eating and drinking? What do these things reveal about the joy and passion of our lives?

It is sin to eat or drink or do anything NOT for the glory of God. In other words, sin is not just a list of harmful things (killing, stealing, etc.). Sin is leaving God out of account in the ordinary affairs of your life. Sin is anything you do that you don't do for the glory of God.¹⁰

DAY 4—BEHOLDING IS BECOMING

God's pleasures do not only relate to our hunger for happiness. They also relate to our transformation into his image.

Examine 2 Corinthians 3:18.

¹⁸And we all, with unveiled face, beholding the glory of the Lord, are being transformed into the same image from one degree of glory to another. For this comes from the Lord who is the Spirit.

Question 7: According to this verse, how are we as human beings changed? Does this change happen only at the final judgment or does it happen throughout our lives?

For the apostle John, the hope of believers is to see the Lord and so be changed, and this future hope significantly impacts our lives in the present. Look now at 1 John 3:1–3.

[1]See what kind of love the Father has given to us, that we should be called children of God; and so we are. The reason why the world does not know us is that it did not know him. [2]Beloved, we are God's children now, and what we will be has not yet appeared; but we know that when he appears we shall be like him, because we shall see him as he is. [3]And everyone who thus hopes in him purifies himself as he is pure.

* **Question 8:** When Christ appears, why will we become like him? How does this relate to our study of the pleasures of God?

We hum the music we listen to. We speak with the accent of our vicinity. We pick up the courtesies of our parents. And we naturally tend to imitate the people we admire most. So it is with God. If we fix our attention on him and hold his glory in our view, we will be changed from one degree of glory to another into his likeness. If teenagers tend to fix their hair like the stars they admire, so Christians will tend to fix their character like the God they admire. In this spiritual transaction seeing is not only believing; seeing is becoming.[11]

DAY 5—WHAT ARE THE PLEASURES OF GOD?

In this study we will seek to understand from the Bible who God is. Many times when theologians examine the doctrine of God, they focus on the attributes of God—his immutability, eternality, righteousness, and power, for example. Rarely do theologians focus on God's pleasures.

* **Question 9:** Why do you think it is important to examine the pleasures of God (as opposed to merely looking at his attributes or character traits)? What advantages are there to seeing God through the lens of his happiness?

There are many things that God delights in. In this DVD study John Piper focuses on six of God's pleasures that provide a clear picture of God's worth and excellency.

Question 10: Look back at the table of contents for this study guide. Which of the pleasures of God mentioned in this study stands out to you the most? Do any of these pleasures surprise you? Explain your answer.

FURTHER UP AND FURTHER IN

Read "What Makes the Good News Good? Seeing the Glory of Christ," an online sermon at the Desiring God website.

> **Question 11:** How would you explain what makes the gospel truly good news after reading this sermon? What keeps us from seeing the glory of Christ?

We have already quoted Henry Scougal's statement on the worth and excellency of the soul. The rest of this quotation is given below.

> The worth and excellency of a soul is to be measured by the object of its love. He who loveth mean and sordid things doth thereby become base and vile, but a noble and well-placed affection doth advance and improve the spirit into a conformity with the perfections which it loves. The images of these do frequently present themselves unto the mind, and, by a secret force and energy, insinuate into the very constitution of the soul and mould and fashion it unto their own likeness.[12]

> **Question 12:** Put this quotation into your own words. Give two examples that illustrate Scougal's argument.

Consider Scougal's expanded definition of the love of God below.

The love of God is a delightful and affectionate sense of the divine perfections which makes the soul resign and sacrifice itself wholly unto him, desiring above all things to please him, and delighting in nothing so much as in fellowship and communion with him, and being ready to do or suffer any thing for his sake or at his pleasure.[13]

Question 13: Notice that Scougal says that we measure the excellency of the soul by the object of its *love*. But we are examining the *pleasures* of God. What exactly is the relationship between pleasure and love? Does love include within it delight and pleasure in the object of love?

Question 14: Many people today regard love as either mere sentimentality or as pure willpower. How does Scougal's definition of love avoid both of these errors?

Read "Loving God for Who He Is: A Pastor's Perspective," an online sermon at the Desiring God website.

Question 15: What is the essence of what it means to love God? How are glorifying God and being satisfied in God related?

—• *While You Watch the DVD, Take Notes* •—

According to John Piper, viewing that God's excellency consists in his well-placed pleasures helps us to do what two things?

_____ is turning away from the source of
_____ and finding it anywhere but in God.

John 17:26: "I made known to them your name, and I will continue to make it known, that the _____ with which
you have _____ me may be in _____, and
I in them.

Seeing God's excellency in his joy transforms me into a
_____ of his excellency.

Therefore, seeing the worth and excellency of God more clearly in
the greatness and the focus of his _____ will help us
to be conformed to his _____ and therefore glorify
him.

—• *After You Watch the DVD, Discuss What You've Learned* •—

1. Discuss John Piper's definition of evil as "turning away from
   the source of happiness," from Jeremiah 2:13. What advantages
   do you see in this definition of evil? What objections might
   someone raise against it?

2. Reread John 15:11 and 17:26. What does it mean for us to
   have God's own joy or love for God *in us*?

3. John Piper says, with reference to 2 Corinthians 3:18, that "beholding means becoming." Discuss any times in your life when you beheld the glory of God and were transformed.

—❖ *After You Discuss, Make Application* ❖—

1. What was the most meaningful part of this lesson for you? Was there a sentence, concept, or idea that really struck you? Why? Record your thoughts in the space below.

2. Pray through Psalm 19:7–11 this week. Thank God for the characteristics of his Word that David describes and ask him to help you feel this way about the Bible more and more. Record your reflections below.

LESSON 4

GOD'S PLEASURE
IN HIS ETERNAL SON

A Companion Study to The Pleasures of God *DVD, Session 3*

LESSON OBJECTIVES

It is our prayer that after you have finished this lesson...
- You will be awakened to the reality that God's highest pleasure is in his Son.
- You will gain a deeper understanding of the Trinity.
- You will see that Jesus is glorious in both his majesty and meekness.

→ *Before You Watch the DVD, Study and Prepare* ←

DAY 1—THE HAPPY GOD

Tucked away in 1 Timothy 1 is an amazing phrase that describes the God of the Bible as the blessed or "happy" God.

Study 1 Timothy 1:8–11.

[8]Now we know that the law is good, if one uses it lawfully, [9]understanding this, that the law is not laid down for the just

but for the lawless and disobedient, for the ungodly and sinners, for the unholy and profane, for those who strike their fathers and mothers, for murderers, [10]the sexually immoral, men who practice homosexuality, enslavers, liars, perjurers, and whatever else is contrary to sound doctrine, [11]in accordance with the gospel of the glory of the blessed God with which I have been entrusted.

* **Question 1:** Reflect upon the description of God in the phrase "the gospel of the glory of the blessed God" (verse 11). What does each word signify? How does each word contribute to the whole phrase? Record your reflections in the space below.

The word translated "blessed" is the Greek word *makarios*. It is used in many other places in the New Testament. "*Blessed* are the poor in spirit, for theirs is the kingdom of heaven" (Matthew 5:3). "It is more *blessed* to give than to receive" (Acts 20:35). "*Blessed* are those whose lawless deeds are forgiven" (Romans 4:7). "Yet in my judgment she is *happier* if she remains as she is" (1 Corinthians 7:40). "[We are] waiting for our *blessed* hope, the appearing of the glory of our great God and Savior Jesus Christ" (Titus 2:13). "*Blessed* are those who are invited to the marriage supper of the Lamb" (Revelation 19:9).

Question 2: In light of these other examples of the word "blessed" (*makarios*), how would you explain the meaning of this word? What synonyms would you use? What does it mean to say "the blessed God"?

DAY 2—THE LOVE OF THE FATHER
FOR THE SON

Why is God blessed or happy? What does God love more than anything else? John 17 is a helpful place to start in answering these questions.

Meditate upon John 17:20–26.

> [20]I do not ask for these only, but also for those who will believe in me through their word, [21]that they may all be one, just as you, Father, are in me, and I in you, that they also may be in us, so that the world may believe that you have sent me. [22]The glory that you have given me I have given to them, that they may be one even as we are one, [23]I in them and you in me, that they may become perfectly one, so that the world may know that you sent me and loved them even as you loved me. [24]Father, I desire that they also, whom you have given me, may be with me where I am, to see my glory that you have given me because you loved me before the foundation of the world. [25]O righteous Father, even though the world does not know you, I know you, and these know that you have sent me. [26]I made known to them your name, and I will continue to make it known, that the love with which you have loved me may be in them, and I in them.

* **Question 3:** How does this text describe the love between the Father and the Son? How long has the Father been loving the Son? According to this passage, what did the Father do because he loved his Son?

Question 4: Why do you think the Father loves the Son? What is it about the Son that brings him such great pleasure? Make a list of all the reasons that you can think of in the space below. If possible, use several biblical texts in your answer.

God is and always has been an exuberantly happy God. From all eternity, even before there were any human beings to love, God has been overflowingly happy in his love for the Son. He has never been lonely. He has always rejoiced, with overflowing satisfaction, in the glory and partnership of his Son.[14]

Day 3—The Majesty of Jesus

Twice in the gospel of Matthew, at Jesus' baptism and at the transfiguration, God the Father declares from heaven that he takes pleasure in his Son.

Study Matthew 17:1–5.

[1]And after six days Jesus took with him Peter and James, and John his brother, and led them up a high mountain by themselves. [2]And he was transfigured before them, and his face shone like the sun, and his clothes became white as light. [3]And behold, there appeared to them Moses and Elijah, talking with him. [4]And Peter said to Jesus, "Lord, it is good that we are here. If you wish, I will make three tents here, one for you and one for Moses and one for Elijah." [5]He was still speaking when, behold, a bright cloud overshadowed them, and a voice from the cloud said, "This is my beloved Son, with whom I am well pleased; listen to him."

* **Question 5:** According to Matthew 17, what happens to Jesus? Why does the Father delight in the Son?

In the apostle Peter's second letter, he reflects on this same event for the benefit of his readers.

Consider 2 Peter 1:16–18.

[16]For we did not follow cleverly devised myths when we made known to you the power and coming of our Lord Jesus Christ, but we were eyewitnesses of his majesty. [17]For when he received honor and glory from God the Father, and the voice was borne to him by the Majestic Glory, "This is my beloved Son, with whom I am well pleased," [18]we ourselves heard this very voice borne from heaven, for we were with him on the holy mountain.

Question 6: Underline every reference to Jesus' majesty in this passage. What different words does Peter use to describe Jesus' transfiguration on the mountain? What did Jesus receive from the Father?

When God declares openly that he loves and delights in his Son, he gives a visual demonstration of the Son's unimaginable glory. His face shone like the sun, his garments became translucent with light, and the disciples fell on their faces (Matthew 17:6). The point is not merely

that humans should stand in awe of such a glory, but that
God himself takes full pleasure in the radiance of his Son.
He reveals him in blinding light, and then says, "This is
my delight!"[15]

DAY 4—THE MEEKNESS OF JESUS

In Matthew 17 we saw that the Father takes great pleasure in the majesty
of the Son. But the transfiguration is not the first time in the gospel that
the Father expresses his delight in the Son.

Meditate on Matthew 3:13–17.

[13]Then Jesus came from Galilee to the Jordan to John, to be
baptized by him. [14]John would have prevented him, saying, "I
need to be baptized by you, and do you come to me?" [15]But Jesus
answered him, "Let it be so now, for thus it is fitting for us to
fulfill all righteousness." Then he consented. [16]And when Jesus
was baptized, immediately he went up from the water, and behold,
the heavens were opened to him, and he saw the Spirit of God
descending like a dove and coming to rest on him; [17]and behold, a
voice from heaven said, "This is my beloved Son, with whom I
am well pleased."

* **Question 7:** How does the Father express his delight in the
    Son in this passage? What does this communicate about
    the reason for the Father's pleasure? How does this compare
    with the Father's delight in the Son at the transfiguration
    (Matthew 17:5)?

The book of Isaiah records several prophecies that find their fulfillment in the ministry of Jesus as the servant of the Lord.

Read Isaiah 42:1–3.

> ¹Behold my servant, whom I uphold, my chosen, in whom my soul delights; I have put my Spirit upon him; he will bring forth justice to the nations. ²He will not cry aloud or lift up his voice, or make it heard in the street; ³a bruised reed he will not break, and a faintly burning wick he will not quench; he will faithfully bring forth justice.

> **Question 8:** This passage from Isaiah is fulfilled in Jesus' ministry in Matthew 12:17–21. According to this passage, why does the servant bring delight to God?

The Father's very soul exults with joy over the servantlike meekness and compassion of his Son. When a reed is bent and about to break, the Servant will tenderly hold it upright until it heals. When a wick is smoldering and has scarcely any heat left, the Servant will not pinch it off, but cup his hand and blow gently until it burns again. Thus the Father cries, "Behold, my Servant in whom my soul delights!"[16]

DAY 5—TWO KINDS OF LOVE

The Bible tells us that God the Father loves the Son and that he loves his people. But does God love Jesus and us the same way or for the same reasons? Consider the following verses.

Study John 3:16, 35; 17:23–24; and 1 John 4:10.

[16]For God so loved the world, that he gave his only Son, that whoever believes in him should not perish but have eternal life. (John 3:16)

[35]The Father loves the Son and has given all things into his hand. (John 3:35)

[23]I in them and you in me, that they may become perfectly one, so that the world may know that you sent me and loved them even as you loved me. [24]Father, I desire that they also, whom you have given me, may be with me where I am, to see my glory that you have given me because you loved me before the foundation of the world. (John 17:23–24)

[10]In this is love, not that we have loved God but that he loved us and sent his Son to be the propitiation for our sins. (1 John 4:10)

* **Question 9:** Underline every use of the word *love* in the verses listed above. In what ways is God's love for the Son similar to his love for his people? In what ways is it different?

Question 10: Do you think that the world deserves God's love (John 3:16)? Why or why not? Do you think 1 John 4:10 describes God's love *because of* the worthiness of the object or God's love *in spite of* the unworthiness of the object? Write your reflections below.

FURTHER UP AND FURTHER IN

Read "The Pleasure of God in His Son," an online sermon at the Desiring God website.

> **Question 11:** In this sermon, John Piper notes that God's pleasure in his Son is a pleasure in himself. To us, this sounds like vanity and conceit. How does Piper respond to the accusation that God is vain if his highest pleasure is in himself reflected in his Son?

> **Question 12:** According to Piper, what is the essence of righteousness?

Read "A Mind in Love with God: The Private Life of a Modern Evangelical," an online message at the Desiring God website.

> **Question 13:** According to Jonathan Edwards, in what two ways is God glorified within himself?

> **Question 14:** How does Piper define virtue in this message? What is the opposite of virtue?

> **Question 15:** Rephrase in your own words how Edwards understood the relationship between God the Father, God the Son,

and God the Holy Spirit. Does this description of the Trinity sound biblical to you? What texts in Scripture might support this view?

—✦ *While You Watch the DVD, Take Notes* ✦—

1 Timothy 1:11: "In accordance with the _____ of the _____ of the _____ God with which I have been entrusted."

God takes pleasure in the divine _____ and _____ of his Son.

The following texts emphasize the *majesty* of Christ.

The following texts emphasize the *meekness* of Christ.

God loves the Son, that is, delights in the Son, with infinite _____ because the Son is the perfect representation and divine radiance of _____.

—✦ *After You Watch the DVD, Discuss What You've Learned* ✦—

1. Is it good news for us that God's highest delight is in his own glory as it is reflected in his Son?

2. Why do you think it is important to emphasize both the similarities *and* the differences between God's love for his Son and God's love for us? What would be lost if we only emphasized the similarities? Only emphasized the differences?

3. Discuss the vision of the Trinity set forth in this message. What is your reaction to this explanation?

→ *After You Discuss, Make Application* ←

1. What was the most meaningful part of this lesson for you? Was there a sentence, concept, or idea that really struck you? Why? Record your thoughts in the space below.

2. Present someone you know with the following two statements and ask her which statement she thinks is more biblical. Based on her answer, attempt to share with her what you have learned in this lesson.
   a. The highest passion of God's heart is human beings.
   b. The highest passion of God's heart is himself. God is the most God-centered person in the universe.

GOD'S PLEASURE IN THE DISPLAY OF HIS GLORY

A Companion Study to The Pleasures of God *DVD, Session 4*

LESSON OBJECTIVES

It is our prayer that after you have finished this lesson…
- You will see the reason why God made the world.
- You will discover what God's most foundational pleasure outside the Trinity is.
- You will understand the relationship between God's holiness and his glory.

—→ Before You Watch the DVD, Study and Prepare ←—

DAY 1—THE GLORY OF GOD BEFORE CREATION

Have you ever stopped to consider what God was doing *before* he created the world? There are several passages of Scripture that give us glimpses into this.

Read John 1:1–2; 17:5; 17:24; and Hebrews 1:3.

[1]In the beginning was the Word, and the Word was with God, and the Word was God. [2]He was in the beginning with God. (John 1:1–2)

[5]And now, Father, glorify me in your own presence with the glory that I had with you before the world existed. (John 17:5)

[24]Father, I desire that they also, whom you have given me, may be with me where I am, to see my glory that you have given me because you loved me before the foundation of the world. (John 17:24)

[3]He is the radiance of the glory of God and the exact imprint of his nature, and he upholds the universe by the word of his power. (Hebrews 1:3)

* **Question 1:** What do these texts tell us about what the Father and the Son were doing before creation? Try to describe their relationship from eternity past.

As John Piper writes, "Before creation the Father and the Son rejoiced in each other with overflowing satisfaction."[17] Jonathan Edwards uses the analogy of a fountain to explain this relationship of overflowing satisfaction. He writes, "Surely it is no argument of the emptiness or deficiency of a fountain, that it is inclined to overflow."[18]

Question 2: How might Edwards's analogy of an overflowing fountain help us to understand why God created the world?

DAY 2—WHY DID GOD CREATE?

Thus far we have emphasized that God is supremely happy in fellowship with his Son. His Son is the radiance of his glory, and the Father takes infinite delight in communion with his most-loved Son. Jonathan Edwards suggests that this infinite fountain of divine delight overflowed in his creation of the world. What does the Bible have to say about God's purpose in creation?

Meditate on Isaiah 43:6–7 and Revelation 4:11.

> ⁶I will say to the north, Give up, and to the south, Do not withhold; bring my sons from afar and my daughters from the end of the earth, ⁷everyone who is called by my name, whom I created for my glory, whom I formed and made. (Isaiah 43:6–7)

> ¹¹Worthy are you, our Lord and God, to receive glory and honor and power, for you created all things, and by your will they existed and were created. (Revelation 4:11)

* Question 3: According to these verses, why did God create?

Question 4: How would you define the term *glory* for someone who was new to the Christian faith? What does it mean to glorify someone or something?

DAY 3—GOD'S GLORY AND HOLINESS

One of the major themes of the book of Leviticus is holiness. The Lord declares five times in this book, "I am holy." What does this word *holy* mean?

Consider Leviticus 11:44–45; 19:2; 20:26; and 21:8.

44For I am the LORD your God. Consecrate yourselves therefore, and be holy, for I am holy. You shall not defile yourselves with any swarming thing that crawls on the ground. 45For I am the LORD who brought you up out of the land of Egypt to be your God. ⸱ You shall therefore be holy, for I am holy. (Leviticus 11:44–45)

2Speak to all the congregation of the people of Israel and say to them, You shall be holy, for I the LORD your God am holy. (Leviticus 19:2)

26You shall be holy to me, for I the LORD am holy and have separated you from the peoples, that you should be mine. (Leviticus 20:26)

8You shall sanctify him, for he offers the bread of your God. He shall be holy to you, for I, the LORD, who sanctify you, am holy. (Leviticus 21:8)

Question 5: What do you think God means when he says, "I am holy"? According to these verses, what is the appropriate response to God's holiness?

In Scripture, God is frequently referred to as holy and as glorious. For example, Exodus 15:11 reads, "Who is like you, O LORD, among the gods? Who is like you, majestic in *holiness,* awesome in *glorious deeds,* doing wonders?" What is the difference between God's holiness and his glory?

Study Isaiah 6:1–5.

¹In the year that King Uzziah died I saw the Lord sitting upon a throne, high and lifted up; and the train of his robe filled the temple. ²Above him stood the seraphim. Each had six wings: with two he covered his face, and with two he covered his feet, and with two he flew. ³And one called to another and said: "Holy, holy, holy is the LORD of hosts; the whole earth is full of his glory!" ⁴And the foundations of the thresholds shook at the voice of him who called, and the house was filled with smoke. ⁵And I said: "Woe is me! For I am lost; for I am a man of unclean lips, and I dwell in the midst of a people of unclean lips; for my eyes have seen the King, the LORD of hosts!"

* **Question 6:** In light of this passage, how would you define God's holiness? What is the relationship between holiness and glory in verse 3?

DAY 4—FOR THE SAKE OF HIS NAME

In Isaiah 43:7, the LORD declares that he created, formed, and made people for his *glory.* But in that very same verse he refers to "everyone who is called by *my name.*" In this passage and throughout the Bible, God's name and God's glory are almost interchangeable terms. The book of Isaiah repeatedly emphasizes God's pursuit of his own glory in his actions.

Examine Isaiah 43:25; 48:9–11; 55:12–13; and 60:21.

> [25]I, I am he who blots out your transgressions for my own sake, and I will not remember your sins. (Isaiah 43:25)

> [9]For my name's sake I defer my anger, for the sake of my praise I restrain it for you, that I may not cut you off. [10]Behold, I have refined you, but not as silver; I have tried you in the furnace of affliction. [11]For my own sake, for my own sake, I do it, for how should my name be profaned? My glory I will not give to another. (Isaiah 48:9–11)

> [12]For you shall go out in joy and be led forth in peace; the mountains and the hills before you shall break forth into singing, and all the trees of the field shall clap their hands. [13]Instead of the thorn shall come up the cypress; instead of the brier shall come up the myrtle; and it shall make a name for the LORD, an everlasting sign that shall not be cut off. (Isaiah 55:12–13)

> [21]Your people shall all be righteous; they shall possess the land forever, the branch of my planting, the work of my hands, that I might be glorified. (Isaiah 60:21)

* **Question 7:** Underline all references to God's name and glory in the verses above, then make a list of the things that God does for the sake of his name and his glory. Record your answer in the space below.

Question 8: Why is it good news for us that God always acts for the sake of his name? Why is it better for us that God acts for his sake and not for our sake when he does all that he does?

DAY 5—FOR THE LORD WILL NOT FORSAKE HIS PEOPLE

We have seen thus far in the lesson that God acts for the sake of his glory, for the sake of his name. We will now examine an important text from the Old Testament where God's commitment to his name is the foundation of his people's hope.

Study 1 Samuel 12:19–25.

[19]And all the people said to Samuel, "Pray for your servants to the LORD your God, that we may not die, for we have added to all our sins this evil, to ask for ourselves a king." [20]And Samuel said to the people, "Do not be afraid; you have done all this evil. Yet do not turn aside from following the LORD, but serve the LORD with all your heart. [21]And do not turn aside after empty things that cannot profit or deliver, for they are empty. [22]For the LORD will not forsake his people, for his great name's sake, because it has pleased the LORD to make you a people for himself. [23]Moreover, as for me, far be it from me that I should sin against the LORD by ceasing to pray for you, and I will instruct you in the good and the right way. [24]Only fear the LORD and serve him faithfully with all your heart. For consider what great things he has done for you. [25]But if you still do wickedly, you shall be swept away, both you and your king.

Question 9: What had the people done for which they deserved to die? What is the reason why Samuel tells the people not to be afraid?

What is the basis of the fearlessness of God's people according to this verse? First of all it is the promise that he will not cast them away. In spite of their sin in wanting a king, the verse says, "The Lord will not cast away his people."

But that is not the deepest foundation of hope and fearlessness in this verse. Why will God not cast away his people? The deepest reason given is in the phrase, "For his great name's sake." The rock bottom foundation of our forgiveness and our fearlessness and our joy is the commitment that God has to his own great name. First, he is committed to act for his own name's sake. And then, for that reason, he is committed to act for his people.[19]

Question 10: Take some time to "consider what great things he has done for you" (verse 24). How does God's being *for you* and not against you (Romans 8:31) relate to his commitment to act for the sake of his name?

FURTHER UP AND FURTHER IN

Read "The Pleasure of God in His Name," an online sermon at the Desiring God website.

Question 11: Explain the "gospel logic" of passages like 1 Samuel 12:19–22 and Psalm 106:7–8.

Question 12: What is the ultimate ground of our hope when everything else has given way?

Read "Is God for Us or for Himself?," an online sermon at the Desiring God website.

Question 13: What purpose drives God in all he does? How is that purpose worked out in redemptive history in events such as the exodus, the exile, and the incarnation?

Question 14: Why is it loving for God to pursue his own glory?

Imagine that explorers recently discovered the world's largest flawless diamond in Russia. The world's leading diamond cutter was called in to cut the diamond, and he presented these perfectly cut, priceless diamonds to the president of Russia in an exquisitely crafted crown. Photographers lined up to take pictures of the presidential crown, and museum curators worldwide salivated at the prospect of attracting huge crowds to see this sui generis diamond collection. But the president of Russia, to everyone's dismay, issued a press release stating that the diamond collection was too valuable to be put on display in museums or even to be photographed for publication, and he had decided to have it hidden and locked in the presidential vault.

Question 15: Do you think that such a valuable diamond collection should be hidden away or publicly displayed? Why or why not? How might this illustration relate to God's decision to publicly display his glory?

—❖ *While You Watch the DVD, Take Notes* ❖—

According to Jonathan Edwards, it is no sign of the deficiency of a fountain that it is prone to _____. That's his explanation for why God _____.

What is the "most foundational pleasure of God outside the Trinity"?

God's _____ is his intrinsic worth; God's _____ is the radiance of that worth.

According to Isaiah 48:9–11, why does God restrain his anger?

The _____ of God is most essentially his acting in a way that upholds and displays his _____.

—❖ *After You Watch the DVD, Discuss What You've Learned* ❖—

1. How would you respond to someone who believed that God created human beings because he was lonely and wanted someone to have fellowship with?

2. Do you agree with Piper when he says that God's God-centeredness is good news for sinners? How would you explain the gospel message to a friend with an emphasis on God's God-centeredness?

3. Discuss any reservations you have about the vision of God's purposes set forth in this lesson.

—•❧ *After You Discuss, Make Application* ❧•—

1. What was the most meaningful part of this lesson for you? Was there a sentence, concept, or idea that really struck you? Why? Record your thoughts in the space below.

2. Piper explained from Isaiah 63:14 that "God's passion for his name is leading him to give you rest like a shepherd." This truth is also found in Psalm 23:3: "He leads me in paths of righteousness for his name's sake." Reflect on the ways that God has led you for his name's sake, and turn Psalm 23:3 into a prayer of thanksgiving.

GOD'S PLEASURE IN ALL THAT HE DOES (PART 1)

A Companion Study to The Pleasures of God *DVD, Session 5*

LESSON OBJECTIVES

It is our prayer that after you have finished this lesson...

- You will be awakened to the glorious truth that God takes great delight in everything he does.
- You will embrace the sovereign freedom of God over nature and over human beings.
- You will find great confidence and security in knowing that an all-sufficient God runs the world.

→✻ *Before You Watch the DVD, Study and Prepare* ✻←

DAY 1—DOES GOD ORDAIN ALL THINGS?

The Westminster Confession of Faith has been an important summary of Christian truth for over three hundred years. The confession contains the following statement about the sovereignty of God.

> God, from all eternity, did, by the most wise and holy counsel of His own will freely, and unchangeably ordain

whatsoever comes to pass: yet so, as thereby neither is God the author of sin, nor is violence offered to the will of the creatures; nor is the liberty or contingency of second causes taken away, but rather established.[20]

Question 1: Rephrase this statement in your own words. Do you agree with this assertion about God's sovereignty? Does God "freely, and unchangeably ordain whatsoever comes to pass"? Explain your answer.

What does the Bible have to say about God's sovereignty and freedom to act how he pleases?

Study Psalm 115:1–3 and Isaiah 46:9–10.

[1]Not to us, O LORD, not to us, but to your name give glory, for the sake of your steadfast love and your faithfulness! [2]Why should the nations say, "Where is their God?" [3]Our God is in the heavens; he does all that he pleases. (Psalm 115:1–3)

[9]Remember the former things of old; for I am God, and there is no other; I am God, and there is none like me, [10]declaring the end from the beginning and from ancient times things not yet done, saying, "My counsel shall stand, and I will accomplish all my purpose." (Isaiah 46:9–10)

* Question 2: According to these passages, what makes God unique and glorious? In light of this, can any of God's purposes be frustrated?

DAY 2—GIVING GIFTS TO GOD

At the end of Romans 11, Paul breaks into an exuberant doxology over the immeasurable wisdom and glory of God in history.

Meditate upon Romans 11:33–36.

> [33]Oh, the depth of the riches and wisdom and knowledge of God! How unsearchable are his judgments and how inscrutable his ways! [34]"For who has known the mind of the Lord, or who has been his counselor?" [35]"Or who has given a gift to him that he might be repaid?" [36]For from him and through him and to him are all things. To him be glory forever. Amen.

Question 3: How would you answer the questions posed in verses 34–35? What is the point of these rhetorical questions?

* **Question 4:** What is the logical connection between verses 34–35 and verse 36? In other words, what is the connection between your answer to Question 3 and the glory of God?

The point is that God acts in sovereign freedom. His acts do not spring from the need to make up deficiencies but from the passion to express the abundance of his delight. This is the meaning of his freedom. I have called it *sovereign* freedom because this is the note that is struck in all three texts we have looked at—God does in fact do all his pleasure. He is free in that he has no deficiencies that make him dependent, and he is sovereign in that he can act on his delights without being stopped by powers outside himself. "All that he pleases, he does." Thus his freedom is a sovereign freedom.[21]

Day 3—God Governs Nature

It is one thing to claim that God always acts in sovereign freedom and that he does all that he pleases. It is another thing to get specific and see all of the areas of life in which God acts in sovereign pleasure.

Study Psalm 135:3–7.

[3]Praise the Lord, for the Lord is good; sing to his name, for it is pleasant! [4]For the Lord has chosen Jacob for himself, Israel as his own possession. [5]For I know that the Lord is great, and that our Lord is above all gods. [6]Whatever the Lord pleases, he does, in heaven and on earth, in the seas and all deeps. [7]He it is who makes the clouds rise at the end of the earth, who makes lightnings for the rain and brings forth the wind from his storehouses.

* **Question 5:** According to Psalm 135, why is God worthy of praise and supreme over all other gods? What examples are given to demonstrate God's sovereign pleasure in all that he does?

The fact that God governs and guides nature is a glorious thing. But it also raises a challenging issue for Christians: If God governs nature according to his good pleasure, does that include natural disasters like storms, tornadoes, and earthquakes?

Question 6: Faced with the question of God's sovereignty over natural disasters, many people attempt to minimize God's control of the natural world. How would you respond to someone who sought to deny that God governs natural phenomena like winds and storms and wild animals? In addition to Psalm 135, what passages of Scripture would you consult?

DAY 4—GOD GOVERNS HUMAN HISTORY

We have seen that God governs nature according to his good pleasure. From the smallest things like the falling of sparrows (Matthew 10:29) to massive things like stars and galaxies (Isaiah 40:26), God "works all things according to the counsel of his will" (Ephesians 1:11). But is God's sovereign freedom limited to nature, or does it also include human history?

Study Daniel 4:34–35 and Proverbs 16:33; 19:21; and 21:1.

> [34] At the end of the days I, Nebuchadnezzar, lifted my eyes to heaven, and my reason returned to me, and I blessed the Most High, and praised and honored him who lives forever, for his dominion is an everlasting dominion, and his kingdom endures from generation to generation; [35] all the inhabitants of the earth are accounted as nothing, and he does according to his will among the host of heaven and among the inhabitants of the earth; and none can stay his hand or say to him, "What have you done?" (Daniel 4:34–35)

> [33] The lot is cast into the lap, but its every decision is from the LORD. (Proverbs 16:33)

²¹Many are the plans in the mind of a man, but it is the purpose of the LORD that will stand. (Proverbs 19:21)

¹The king's heart is a stream of water in the hand of the LORD; he turns it wherever he will. (Proverbs 21:1)

* Question 7: In light of these passages, how does God's sovereignty relate to the actions and decisions of human beings? Explain your answer below.

The fact that God does according to his will among the host of heaven and the inhabitants of the earth is gloriously true. But again, it also raises the complex question of God's sovereignty over the evil actions of men.

Question 8: Do you believe that God guides, governs, plans, and directs the actions of human beings, even the wicked actions of evil men? What examples could you give from Scripture to substantiate your position?

DAY 5—IS GOD OUR MODEL RISK TAKER?

Some Christian theologians have presented God as our model risk taker. They explain that God took a risk in creating the world where people are given free will. He took a risk in the incarnation of his Son, since Herod's soldiers could have killed Jesus while he was still a baby. He took a risk when he entrusted the church with the Great Commission, because the church could fail in its responsibility to preach the gospel to all the nations. The argument goes that since God takes risks, we should be inspired to do the same and risk our lives for him.

> **Question 9:** Do you find this explanation of God as a risk taker compelling? What does it mean for someone to take risks? Explain your answer below.

Why is there such a thing as risk? The reason there is such a thing as risk is that there is such a thing as ignorance. If there were no ignorance, there would be no risk. Risk is possible because we don't know how things will turn out. This means that God can take no risks. He knows the outcome of all his choices before they happen. And since he knows the outcome of all his actions before they happen, he plans accordingly. His omniscience rules out the very possibility of taking risks. But not so with us. We are not God; we are ignorant. We don't know what will happen tomorrow.[22]

According to John Piper, to describe God as a risk taker "calls into question his omniscience and sovereignty, and therefore takes away the very foundation of our confidence, and thus the power that enables us to take risks for God."[23] Consider these words from Patrick Johnstone:

Only the Lamb could open the seals. All the earth-shaking awesome forces unleashed on the world are released by the Lord Jesus Christ. He reigns today. He is in the control room of the universe. He is the only Ultimate Cause;

all the sins of man and machinations of Satan ultimately have to enhance the glory and kingdom of our Saviour. This is true of our world today—in wars, famines, earthquakes, or the evil that apparently has the ascendancy. All God's actions are just and loving. We have become too enemy-conscious, and can over-do the spiritual warfare aspect of intercession. We need to become more God-conscious, so that we can laugh the laugh of faith knowing that we have power over all the power of the enemy (Luke 10:19). He has already lost control because of Calvary where the Lamb was slain. What confidence and rest of heart this gives us as we face a world in turmoil and in such spiritual need.[24]

* **Question 10:** How does God's sovereign control of all things relate to our taking risks for the spread of the gospel in the world?

Further Up and Further In

Read "The Pleasure of God in All That He Does," an online sermon at the Desiring God website.

Question 11: What assumptions does Piper make that serve as the foundation for this sermon?

Question 12: Do you believe that God is *always* infinitely happy? Is he ever frustrated or disappointed? Explain your answer.

Question 13: Why do you think that some people want to limit God's sovereignty to the natural world? Why will limiting God in this way not solve the problem that they are seeking to address?

Read "Risk and the Cause of God," an online sermon at the Desiring God website.

Question 14: What are some examples of people who have taken risks for the cause of God?

Question 15: How does Piper help us to explode the myth of safety and security?

—❖ *While You Watch the DVD, Take Notes* ❖—

An essential aspect of God's glory is his _____ to do all that he pleases.

What is an essential difference between God and us?

What is glorious about God specifically from Romans 11:33–36?

What passages of Scripture show that God's invisible hand is behind all that comes to pass?

According to Piper, we should feel massively _____ that an all- _____ God runs the world.

→❈ *After You Watch the DVD, Discuss What You've Learned* ❈←

1. Discuss the biblical teaching on the sovereignty of God. Interact with the following statement: God is pleased to govern, guide, and ordain all things in the universe. He "works all things according to the counsel of his will" (Ephesians 1:11).

2. How could you use the doctrine of God's sovereign freedom to do all that he pleases to encourage someone who is suffering?

3. How does prayer fit in with this teaching about God's sovereignty? Why was it wrong for John Piper's grandmother to say that she didn't want to bother God with her little concerns?

—* *After You Discuss, Make Application* *—

1. What was the most meaningful part of this lesson for you? Was there a sentence, concept, or idea that really struck you? Why? Record your thoughts in the space below.

2. Reflect on Isaiah 40:28–31. Why is God's sovereign power good news to his people? Think of someone who is going through a difficult trial whom you can encourage with this text, and take some time to pray for that person.

LESSON 7

GOD'S PLEASURE IN ALL THAT HE DOES (PART 2)

A Companion Study to The Pleasures of God *DVD, Session 6*

LESSON OBJECTIVES

It is our prayer that after you have finished this lesson...
- You will be able to embrace the vision of God's providence that Joseph had in Genesis 50:20.
- You will understand the distinction between God's secret and revealed wills.
- You will begin to grasp the depths of the complexity of God's emotional life.

—⟶ *Before You Watch the DVD, Study and Prepare* ⟵—

DAY 1—GOD MEANT IT FOR GOOD

The account of Joseph in Genesis 37–50 is one of the most familiar and important stories of God's providence in the Bible. The narrative reaches a climax in chapter 50, when Jacob dies and Joseph's brothers fear that Joseph, now a very powerful leader in Egypt, will exact revenge on them for their earlier sins against him. Joseph's response to his brothers is surprising, and it is explainable only by his strong belief in the sovereign goodness of God.

Consider Genesis 50:15–21.

[15]When Joseph's brothers saw that their father was dead, they said, "It may be that Joseph will hate us and pay us back for all the evil that we did to him." [16]So they sent a message to Joseph, saying, "Your father gave this command before he died, [17]'Say to Joseph, Please forgive the transgression of your brothers and their sin, because they did evil to you.' And now, please forgive the transgression of the servants of the God of your father." Joseph wept when they spoke to him. [18]His brothers also came and fell down before him and said, "Behold, we are your servants." [19]But Joseph said to them, "Do not fear, for am I in the place of God? [20]As for you, you meant evil against me, but God meant it for good, to bring it about that many people should be kept alive, as they are today. [21]So do not fear; I will provide for you and your little ones." Thus he comforted them and spoke kindly to them.

Question 1: What had Joseph's brothers done to him earlier in the story (review Genesis 37:12–36)? How is this treatment of Joseph by his brothers described in this passage?

* Question 2: Why does Joseph tell his brothers not to fear in Genesis 50:19, 21? What sort of perspective does Joseph bring to the situation with his brothers? How does Joseph describe God's intention and purpose in what happened to him?

The brothers meant the sale of Joseph for evil, but God meant it for good. Notice it does not say that God used their evil for good after they meant it for evil. It says that in the very act of evil, there were two different designs: In the sinful act, they were designing evil, and in the same sinful act, God was designing good.

This is what we have seen and will see over and over: What man designs—or the devil designs—for evil, God designs for some great good. The great good mentioned in Genesis 45:5 is "to preserve life." And the great good mentioned in Genesis 50:20 is "to bring it about that many people should be kept alive, as they are today." But in those words, and the whole story of how God saves his people, are pointers to the global purpose of this sin—this life-saving sin—in the glory of Jesus Christ.[25]

Day 2—Both Good and Bad

It is easy to say that God is behind good gifts and blessings in our lives, but it is much harder to say that God has wise, sovereign designs when calamity strikes. When Satan appears before God in Job 1:9, he appeals to God's blessing Job and asks, "Does Job fear God for no reason?" Satan challenges the Lord to stretch out his hand and touch all that he has, and he predicts that Job will curse God when faced with calamity.

Study Job 2:6–10.

[6]And the Lord said to Satan, "Behold, he is in your hand; only spare his life." [7]So Satan went out from the presence of the Lord and struck Job with loathsome sores from the sole of his foot to the crown of his head. [8]And he took a piece of broken pottery with which to scrape himself while he sat in the ashes. [9]Then his wife said to him, "Do you still hold fast your integrity? Curse God

and die." [10]But he said to her, "You speak as one of the foolish women would speak. Shall we receive good from God, and shall we not receive evil?" In all this Job did not sin with his lips.

* **Question 3:** What painful trial befalls Job in this passage? Who is behind this trial according to the narrator? according to Job's wife? according to Job?

Comforts and calamities come from the hand of God. This rock solid confidence in the sovereignty of God Job will not relinquish—and neither should we! Picture Satan in heaven surrounded by 10,000 angels awaiting Job's response. Then Job answers, and, unknown to him, 20,000 arms are raised and 10,000 mighty voices shout, "Worthy is the Lord God of Job!" And what does Satan do? He flees from the presence of the praise of God.[26]

Meditate on Lamentations 3:37–38 and Isaiah 45:7.

[37]Who has spoken and it came to pass, unless the Lord has commanded it? [38]Is it not from the mouth of the Most High that good and bad come? (Lamentations 3:37–38)

[7]I form light and create darkness, I make well-being and create calamity, I am the LORD, who does all these things. (Isaiah 45:7)

Question 4: What is the expected answer to these questions in Lamentations 3:37–38? What actions does the Lord command or do in these passages?

Day 3—The Complexity of God's Emotional Life

Thus far in our study we have seen that God acts in sovereign freedom to do according to his pleasure in relation to nature and in relation to human beings. Therefore, God does, in fact, take pleasure in all that he does. But is the answer that simple?

Reflect upon Ezekiel 18:30–32.

> [30]Therefore I will judge you, O house of Israel, every one according to his ways, declares the Lord God. Repent and turn from all your transgressions, lest iniquity be your ruin. [31]Cast away from you all the transgressions that you have committed, and make yourselves a new heart and a new spirit! Why will you die, O house of Israel? [32]For I have no pleasure in the death of anyone, declares the Lord God; so turn, and live.

From this passage it would seem that there are some things (like the death of the wicked) that God does not take pleasure in. But again, the issue is not that simple.

Study Deuteronomy 28:63.

> [63]And as the Lord took delight in doing you good and multiplying you, so the Lord will take delight in bringing ruin upon you and destroying you. And you shall be plucked off the land that you are entering to take possession of it.

Question 5: What tension do you notice between Ezekiel 18:32 and Deuteronomy 28:63 in how they describe God's pleasure? Attempt to resolve this tension in the space below.

As we can see, the question of God's delight in *everything* he does, including destroying the wicked, is very complex. Another way to see this complexity is by examining biblical descriptions of God's emotional life.

Study Psalm 149:4; Luke 15:7; Ephesians 4:30; and Psalm 7:11.

> [4]For the LORD takes pleasure in his people; he adorns the humble with salvation. (Psalm 149:4)

> [7]Just so, I tell you, there will be more joy in heaven over one sinner who repents than over ninety-nine righteous persons who need no repentance. (Luke 15:7)

> [30]And do not grieve the Holy Spirit of God, by whom you were sealed for the day of redemption. (Ephesians 4:30)

> [11]God is a righteous judge, and a God who feels indignation every day. (Psalm 7:11)

* **Question 6:** Based on these passages, what picture of God's emotional life emerges? Is God rejoicing and delighting, or grieved and angry? How often does God feel these emotions?

DAY 4—GOD'S TWO WILLS

Faithful interpreters of the Bible have noticed that when the Bible speaks of God's *purpose* or *will*, it could refer to his revealed, moral will for his people, as in 1 Thessalonians 5:16–18: "Rejoice always, pray without ceasing, give thanks in all circumstances; for this is *the will of God* in Christ Jesus for you." But at other times in Scripture, God's will refers to his sovereign, secret decree, as in Isaiah 46:10: "Declaring the end from the beginning and from ancient times things not yet done, saying, 'My counsel shall stand, and I will accomplish all *my purpose.*'" This distinction in God's two wills is set forth in Deuteronomy 29:29: "*The secret things* belong to the LORD our God, but *the things that are revealed* belong to us and to our children forever, that we may do all the words of this law." This framework helps us to interpret passages where God's secret and revealed wills appear to be opposed, as in the crucifixion of the Son of God.

Study Acts 2:23 and 4:27–28.

23This Jesus, delivered up according to the definite plan and foreknowledge of God, you crucified and killed by the hands of lawless men. (Acts 2:23)

27For truly in this city there were gathered together against your holy servant Jesus, whom you anointed, both Herod and Pontius Pilate, along with the Gentiles and the peoples of Israel, 28to do whatever your hand and your plan had predestined to take place. (Acts 4:27–28)

* **Question 7:** How do these two passages describe, on the one hand, the will of Jesus' opponents and, on the other hand, the will of God in the crucifixion? Which of God's wills is carried out in the death of Jesus: his revealed, moral will or his sovereign, secret decree?

Herod, Pilate, the soldiers and Jewish crowds lifted their hand to rebel against the Most High only to find that their rebellion was unwitting (sinful) service in the inscrutable designs of God.... Therefore we know it was not the "will of God" that Judas and Pilate and Herod and the Gentile soldiers and the Jewish crowds disobey the moral law of God by sinning in delivering Jesus up to be crucified. But we also know that it was the will of God that this come to pass. Therefore we know that God in some sense wills what he does not will in another sense.[27]

Several passages of Scripture clearly teach that God desires that people repent of their sins, believe in Christ, and be saved. Yet other passages of Scripture teach that only those whom God has sovereignly chosen will be saved. Consider the following biblical texts as you wrestle through this question.

Read John 6:40, 44; Ephesians 1:4–6; and 1 Timothy 2:3–4; 4:10.

[40]For this is the will of my Father, that everyone who looks on the Son and believes in him should have eternal life, and I will raise him up on the last day. (John 6:40)

[44]No one can come to me unless the Father who sent me draws him. And I will raise him up on the last day. (John 6:44)

[4]Even as he chose us in him before the foundation of the world, that we should be holy and blameless before him. In love [5]he predestined us for adoption as sons through Jesus Christ, according to the purpose of his will, [6]to the praise of his glorious grace, with which he has blessed us in the Beloved. (Ephesians 1:4–6)

[3]This is good, and it is pleasing in the sight of God our Savior, [4]who desires all people to be saved and to come to the knowledge of the truth. (1 Timothy 2:3–4)

[10]For to this end we toil and strive, because we have our hope set on the living God, who is the Savior of all people, especially of those who believe. (1 Timothy 4:10)

Question 8: What do these verses say about God's revealed will and desire that all be saved? What do these verses say about God's secret, sovereign decree in electing and calling some people to salvation?

Day 5—The Heart of Pharaoh and the Glory of God

Israel's exodus from slavery in Egypt is one of the most important events in the Bible, as God reveals himself as "the Lord your God, who brought you out of the land of Egypt, out of the house of slavery" (Exodus 20:2). The Lord not only brings his people out of Egypt, he demonstrates that he is supreme over Egypt and Pharaoh and sovereign over human hearts. Consider the following texts that reference the hardening of Pharaoh's heart.

Read Exodus 4:21; 7:13; 9:12, 34; 10:1–2; and 14:17.

[21]And the Lord said to Moses, "When you go back to Egypt, see that you do before Pharaoh all the miracles that I have put in your power. But I will harden his heart, so that he will not let the people go." (Exodus 4:21)

[13]Still Pharaoh's heart was hardened, and he would not listen to them, as the Lord had said. (Exodus 7:13)

[12]But the LORD hardened the heart of Pharaoh, and he did not listen to them, as the LORD had spoken to Moses. (Exodus 9:12)

[34]But when Pharaoh saw that the rain and the hail and the thunder had ceased, he sinned yet again and hardened his heart, he and his servants. (Exodus 9:34)

[1]Then the LORD said to Moses, "Go in to Pharaoh, for I have hardened his heart and the heart of his servants, that I may show these signs of mine among them, [2]and that you may tell in the hearing of your son and of your grandson how I have dealt harshly with the Egyptians and what signs I have done among them, that you may know that I am the LORD." (Exodus 10:1–2)

[17]And I will harden the hearts of the Egyptians so that they shall go in after them, and I will get glory over Pharaoh and all his host, his chariots, and his horsemen. (Exodus 14:17)

* **Question 9:** According to these texts, did Pharaoh harden his own heart or did the Lord harden Pharaoh's heart? Did Pharaoh carry out the revealed, moral will of God? Did he carry out the sovereign, secret will of God? What is the purpose behind the hardening of Pharaoh's heart?

The apostle Paul uses the hardening of Pharaoh's heart as an example of God's freedom to have mercy and his freedom to harden.

Read Romans 9:16–18.

[16]So then it depends not on human will or exertion, but on God, who has mercy. [17]For the Scripture says to Pharaoh, "For this

very purpose I have raised you up, that I might show my power
in you, and that my name might be proclaimed in all the earth."
[18]So then he has mercy on whomever he wills, and he hardens
whomever he wills.

Question 10: What was God's purpose in raising up Pharaoh to
his position? How does the story of Pharaoh's hardening illustrate God's sovereign freedom?

Now we see why Paul chose to quote Exodus 9:16 in
Romans 9:17 rather than one of the verses that relate
directly to hardening.... He chose a verse that expressed
the very purpose that relates implicitly to the righteousness of God and the hope of the world: namely, God's
commitment to uphold and display the honor of his
name—"that my name might be proclaimed in all the
earth." In other words, God's freedom in mercy and
hardening is at the heart of God's glory and God's name.
This is what it means to be God—to be ultimately free
and unconstrained from powers outside himself. Treasur-
ing and displaying this glory and this name is right—it is
the meaning of "right." And it is God's purpose for the
whole earth. He will reveal it to the whole earth.[28]

Further Up and Further In

**Read "Are There Two Wills in God?," an online article at the Desir-
ing God website.**

Question 11: What is John Piper's aim in this article? What "two wills" does God have that coexist and are not contradictory?

Question 12: What is the clearest example of God's willing for sin to come to pass while at the same time disapproving the sin? What other examples of this pattern can you think of from Scripture?

Question 13: What does God will more than saving all people? What is his highest commitment?

Read "The Sale of Joseph and the Son of God," an online sermon at the Desiring God website.

Question 14: In what way is the story of Joseph a fulfillment of God's covenant promises and prophecy given to Abraham? What are two biblical descriptions of this fulfillment?

Question 15: In what ways does the story of Joseph prepare us to see the glory of Christ?

—*» *While You Watch the DVD, Take Notes* «*—

Genesis 50:20: "As for you, you _____ evil against me,
   but God _____ it for good, to bring it about that
   many people should be kept alive." What is *the issue* for us
   when we go through hard, painful trials while knowing that
   God has a design in each situation?

Texts like Lamentations 3:37 show us that the Old Testament
   writers inspired by God were simply absorbed in the
   _____ of God.
How does the Bible describe the emotional life of God?

According to Piper, God has _____ of willing and
   delighting.

—*» *After You Watch the DVD, Discuss What You've Learned* «*—

1. Put yourself in Joseph's place when he addressed his brothers
   who sold him into slavery years before. Do you think you
   could say what he said in Genesis 50:20? Why or why not?

2. Think of an example where you experienced two seemingly
   contradictory emotions in the same circumstance. Then think
   of an example where God was both approving and
   disapproving of something at the same time.

3. What is your response to what Piper calls "the complexity of God's emotional life"? Are you persuaded by his resolution to this biblical tension? Are there any other ways to resolve this tension?

—→ *After You Discuss, Make Application* ←—

1. What was the most meaningful part of this lesson for you? Was there a sentence, concept, or idea that really struck you? Why? Record your thoughts in the space below.

2. Reflect on the promise of Romans 8:28: "And we know that for those who love God all things work together for good, for those who are called according to his purpose." How does the story of Joseph illustrate this promise? Think of a testimony from your own life where God was at work for good in a difficult or painful trial.

GOD'S PLEASURE IN ALL OF CREATION (PART 1)

A Companion Study to The Pleasures of God *DVD, Session 7*

LESSON OBJECTIVES

It is our prayer that after you have finished this lesson...
- You will marvel at the goodness of God's creation.
- You will begin to use God's material creation as a springboard for worship.
- You will see that the incarnation of Jesus depicts God's pleasure in creation.

→* ***Before You Watch the DVD, Study and Prepare*** *←—

DAY 1—IT WAS VERY GOOD!

The previous lessons have focused on the pleasure God has in his Son, in the display of his glory, and in all that he does. We now turn to examine God's pleasure in his creation.

Read Genesis 1:4, 12, 17–18, 21, 25, 31.

⁴And God saw that the light was good. And God separated the light from the darkness....

¹²The earth brought forth vegetation, plants yielding seed according to their own kinds, and trees bearing fruit in which is their seed, each according to its kind. And God saw that it was good....

¹⁷And God set them [the sun and the moon] in the expanse of the heavens to give light on the earth, ¹⁸to rule over the day and over the night, and to separate the light from the darkness. And God saw that it was good....

²¹So God created the great sea creatures and every living creature that moves, with which the waters swarm, according to their kinds, and every winged bird according to its kind. And God saw that it was good....

²⁵And God made the beasts of the earth according to their kinds and the livestock according to their kinds, and everything that creeps on the ground according to its kind. And God saw that it was good....

³¹And God saw everything that he had made, and behold, it was very good. And there was evening and there was morning, the sixth day.

* **Question 1:** Underline every reference to the goodness of God's creation in the passage above. What parts of creation are called good? Why do you think the theme of creation's goodness is repeated so much in Genesis 1?

I take this to mean at least that God was delighted with his work. He approved of it. He was glad that he had done it. When he looked at it, it gave him pleasure. It is as though he said, "Yes, that's it. That will do just fine. That's exactly right." And we get the clue early on in the story that the root of his delight in creation has to do with imaging forth his own glory, because only after he created man and woman in his image did God add the word "very" to the word "good."[29]

Reflect upon Job 38:1–7.

[1]Then the LORD answered Job out of the whirlwind and said: [2]"Who is this that darkens counsel by words without knowledge? [3]Dress for action like a man; I will question you, and you make it known to me. [4]Where were you when I laid the foundation of the earth? Tell me, if you have understanding. [5]Who determined its measurements—surely you know! Or who stretched the line upon it? [6]On what were its bases sunk, or who laid its cornerstone, [7]when the morning stars sang together and all the sons of God shouted for joy?"

Question 2: What is the Lord's point in his answer to Job here? What evidence is there from this passage for God's pleasure in creation?

DAY 2—CREATION IS A POEM ABOUT GOD

There are certain things that are true for all people at all times. All people eat food and drink water; all people see the sun rise and set; they feel the wind blow and the rain fall. According to the apostle Paul, these "natural" things in life are communicating something profound about the Creator God.

Study Romans 1:18–20.

[18]For the wrath of God is revealed from heaven against all ungodliness and unrighteousness of men, who by their unrighteousness suppress the truth. [19]For what can be known about God is plain to them, because God has shown it to them. [20]For his invisible attributes, namely, his eternal power and divine nature, have been clearly perceived, ever since the creation of the world, in the things that have been made. So they are without excuse.

* **Question 3:** According to these verses, what is revealed about God in creation? What sort of knowledge of God does revelation in creation bring about?

What does he do to make himself evident? He made the world. He created—like a potter, or a sculptor or a poet, except he created out of nothing. In verse 20, when it says that God is "understood through what has been made," the words "what has been made" stand for one Greek word (which you will all recognize), the word *poiema*. It's the word from which we get "poem." The universe and everything in it is God's work of art. What's the point of this word? The point is that in a poem there is manifest design and intention and wisdom and power. The wind might create a letter in the sand, but not a poem. That's the point. God acted. God planned. God designed. God crafted. He created and made. And in doing that, Paul says in verse 19, God made himself evident to all mankind. The universe is a poem about God.[30]

Question 4: What is true of all people because of God's revelation in creation?

Day 3—A Wrong Response to Creation

We have already seen that the universe is a poem about God that gives all people sufficient revelation of God's power and nature, such that they are without excuse. Paul goes on in the next verses of Romans 1 to explain how humanity has responded to God's revelation in creation.

Meditate on Romans 1:20–25.

[20]For his invisible attributes, namely, his eternal power and divine nature, have been clearly perceived, ever since the creation of the world, in the things that have been made. So they are without excuse. [21]For although they knew God, they did not honor him as God or give thanks to him, but they became futile in their thinking, and their foolish hearts were darkened. [22]Claiming to be wise, they became fools, [23]and exchanged the glory of the immortal God for images resembling mortal man and birds and animals and creeping things. [24]Therefore God gave them up in the lusts of their hearts to impurity, to the dishonoring of their bodies among themselves, [25]because they exchanged the truth about God for a lie and worshiped and served the creature rather than the Creator, who is blessed forever! Amen.

* **Question 5:** What should the knowledge of God lead people to do? What have they done instead? What does Paul say that people have "exchanged"?

Consider Isaiah 44:10–11 and 18–22.

[10]Who fashions a god or casts an idol that is profitable for nothing? [11]Behold, all his companions shall be put to shame, and the craftsmen are only human. Let them all assemble, let them stand forth. They shall be terrified; they shall be put to shame together.... [18]They know not, nor do they discern, for he has shut their eyes, so that they cannot see, and their hearts, so that they cannot understand. [19]No one considers, nor is there knowledge or discernment to say, "Half of it I burned in the fire; I also baked bread on its coals; I roasted meat and have eaten. And shall I make the rest of it an abomination? Shall I fall down before a block of wood?" [20]He feeds on ashes; a deluded heart has led him astray, and he cannot deliver himself or say, "Is there not a lie in my right hand?"

[21]Remember these things, O Jacob, and Israel, for you are my servant; I formed you; you are my servant; O Israel, you will not be forgotten by me. [22]I have blotted out your transgressions like a cloud and your sins like mist; return to me, for I have redeemed you.

Question 6: According to Isaiah 44, why is it foolish to worship and serve "the creature rather than the Creator," as Paul says in Romans 1:25? What does the Lord want his people to remember about him and how he differs from other so-called gods?

DAY 4—MORE SPIRITUAL THAN GOD

After reading texts such as Romans 1 and Isaiah 44, some might assume that creation and the pleasure that it brings poses too much of a temptation to idolatry to still be "good." From the beginning there have been some who have struggled with how to relate to the material world, as the following texts show.

Study 1 Timothy 4:1–5.

> ¹Now the Spirit expressly says that in later times some will depart from the faith by devoting themselves to deceitful spirits and teachings of demons, ²through the insincerity of liars whose consciences are seared, ³who forbid marriage and require abstinence from foods that God created to be received with thanksgiving by those who believe and know the truth. ⁴For everything created by God is good, and nothing is to be rejected if it is received with thanksgiving, ⁵for it is made holy by the word of God and prayer.

* **Question 7:** According to this passage, what is the demonic teaching that will spread in later times? Underline every place that it appears. What is the biblical response to this demonic teaching?

Consider Colossians 2:18–23.

> ¹⁸Let no one disqualify you, insisting on asceticism and worship of angels, going on in detail about visions, puffed up without reason by his sensuous mind, ¹⁹and not holding fast to the Head,

from whom the whole body, nourished and knit together
through its joints and ligaments, grows with a growth that is
from God. [20]If with Christ you died to the elemental spirits of
the world, why, as if you were still alive in the world, do you
submit to regulations— [21]"Do not handle, Do not taste, Do
not touch" [22](referring to things that all perish as they are
used)—according to human precepts and teachings? [23]These
have indeed an appearance of wisdom in promoting self-made
religion and asceticism and severity to the body, but they are
of no value in stopping the indulgence of the flesh.

Question 8: What similarities do you see between Colossians 2
and 1 Timothy 4? According to this passage, what is the
fundamental problem with asceticism?

There is no use trying to be more spiritual than God. God
never meant man to be a purely spiritual creature. That is
why He uses material things like bread and wine to put
the new life into us. We may think this rather crude and
unspiritual. God does not: He invented eating. He likes
matter. He invented it....
  I know some muddleheaded Christians have talked
as if Christianity thought that sex, or the body, or pleasure, were bad in themselves. But they were wrong.
Christianity is almost the only one of the great religions
which thoroughly approves of the body—which believes
that matter is good, that God Himself once took on a
human body, and that some kind of body is going to be
given to us even in Heaven and is going to be an essential part of our happiness, our beauty, and our energy.[31]

DAY 5—THE CREATOR BECAME A MAN

According to C. S. Lewis, one of the strongest arguments for why Christians should not reject the material world is the fact that "God Himself once took on a human body." What does the incarnation tell us about God's pleasure in creation?

Consider John 1:1–3, 14; Philippians 2:5–7; and Hebrews 2:14.

> [1]In the beginning was the Word, and the Word was with God, and the Word was God. [2]He was in the beginning with God. [3]All things were made through him, and without him was not any thing made that was made.... [14]And the Word became flesh and dwelt among us, and we have seen his glory, glory as of the only Son from the Father, full of grace and truth. (John 1:1–3, 14)

> [5]Have this mind among yourselves, which is yours in Christ Jesus, [6]who, though he was in the form of God, did not count equality with God a thing to be grasped, [7]but made himself nothing, taking the form of a servant, being born in the likeness of men. (Philippians 2:5–7)

> [14]Since therefore the children share in flesh and blood, he himself likewise partook of the same things, that through death he might destroy the one who has the power of death, that is, the devil. (Hebrews 2:14)

* **Question 9:** Underline all references to the incarnation in these verses. What are some of the reasons why Jesus the Creator took on human flesh?

What sort of body did Jesus have after he rose from the dead? When he ascended into heaven (Acts 1:9), did Jesus give up his human body or is he still fully God and fully man? What sort of body will believers have in the new heavens and new earth?

Study Luke 24:36–43; Romans 6:5; and Philippians 3:20–21.

36As they were talking about these things, Jesus himself stood among them, and said to them, "Peace to you!" 37But they were startled and frightened and thought they saw a spirit. 38And he said to them, "Why are you troubled, and why do doubts arise in your hearts? 39See my hands and my feet, that it is I myself. Touch me, and see. For a spirit does not have flesh and bones as you see that I have." 40And when he had said this, he showed them his hands and his feet. 41And while they still disbelieved for joy and were marveling, he said to them, "Have you anything here to eat?" 42They gave him a piece of broiled fish, 43and he took it and ate before them. (Luke 24:36–43)

5For if we have been united with him in a death like his, we shall certainly be united with him in a resurrection like his. (Romans 6:5)

20But our citizenship is in heaven, and from it we await a Savior, the Lord Jesus Christ, 21who will transform our lowly body to be like his glorious body, by the power that enables him even to subject all things to himself. (Philippians 3:20–21)

Question 10: How does Luke 24 describe Jesus' body after he rose from the dead? According to Romans 6 and Philippians 3, what is the relationship between Jesus' body and our body?

Further Up and Further In

Read "The Pleasure of God in His Creation," an online sermon at the Desiring God website.

> **Question 11:** What biblical texts support the claim that God takes pleasure in his creation?

> **Question 12:** What are five reasons why God takes pleasure in his creation?

Read "Displays of God Remove the Excuse for Failed Worship," an online sermon at the Desiring God website.

> **Question 13:** Why are all people without excuse for failing to worship God as they ought?

> **Question 14:** According to Romans 1, what sort of knowledge of God do all people have? How is it that even nonbelievers can "know God" (verses 19–21, 32)?

> **Question 15:** What essential problem with the theory of naturalistic evolution is addressed in this sermon?

—•» *While You Watch the DVD, Take Notes* «•—

God is not easy to understand in his _____, but he is all
    we need in our _____.
What are some implications of God's pleasure in all that he does?

What are God's plans for the created world?

C. S. Lewis wrote, "There is no use trying to be more spiritual than
    God. God never meant man to be a purely _____
    creature. That is why He uses _____ things like
    bread and wine to put the new life into us. We may think this
    rather crude and unspiritual. God does not: He invented eat-
    ing. He likes matter. He invented it."
How did God intend for believers to respond to pleasures like sex
    and food?

—•» *After You Watch the DVD, Discuss What You've Learned* «•—

1. Discuss specific ways that you can use creation to worship God
    more fully.

2. Think of a time when you were amazed at God's design in creation. What about it amazed you? Be specific and share with the group.

3. Do you find that you personally are more tempted to idolize or demonize the created world?

→✵ *After You Discuss, Make Application* ✵←

1. What was the most meaningful part of this lesson for you? Was there a sentence, concept, or idea that really struck you? Why? Record your thoughts in the space below.

2. Meditate on 1 Timothy 4:4: "For everything created by God is good, and nothing is to be rejected if it is received with thanksgiving." Write down some evidences of God's goodness in creation. Then write down some reasons that you are thankful for God's wisdom and generosity in the things that he has made.

GOD'S PLEASURE IN ALL OF CREATION (PART 2)

A Companion Study to The Pleasures of God *DVD, Session 8*

LESSON OBJECTIVES

It is our prayer that after you have finished this lesson...

- You will grasp the distinction between the glory of creation and the glory of God.
- You will consider how to love good and pleasurable things in creation for God's sake.
- You will be moved to worship God through both feasting and fasting.

—•> *Before You Watch the DVD, Study and Prepare* <•—

DAY 1—THE TESTIMONY OF THE HEAVENS

Think of a time when you have been outside of the city and away from all man-made lighting and have looked up at a clear night sky. The brilliance of the stars as far as you can see is truly majestic. Or consider the fact that as the earth orbits the sun and turns on its axis, the sun rises and sets every day again and again and again. The psalmist reflects on what these amazing wonders of the heavens tell us about our great Creator.

Meditate on Psalm 19:1–6.

> [1]The heavens declare the glory of God, and the sky above proclaims his handiwork. [2]Day to day pours out speech, and night to night reveals knowledge. [3]There is no speech, nor are there words, whose voice is not heard. [4]Their voice goes out through all the earth, and their words to the end of the world. In them he has set a tent for the sun, [5]which comes out like a bridegroom leaving his chamber, and, like a strong man, runs its course with joy. [6]Its rising is from the end of the heavens, and its circuit to the end of them, and there is nothing hidden from its heat.

* **Question 1:** According to this passage, what is the testimony of the heavens that God has created? What is the relationship between the glory of *creation* and the glory of *God*?

It is clear that there is one main message creation has to communicate to human beings, namely, the glory of God. Not primarily the glory of creation, but the glory of God. The glory of creation and the glory of God are as different as the love poem and the love, the painting and the landscape, the ring and the marriage. It would be a great folly and a great tragedy if a man loved his wedding band more than he loved his bride.[32]

We have looked at the opening six verses of Psalm 19, which stress the testimony of day and night that God is glorious. In verses 7–11, David considers the perfect and sufficient testimony of the law of God and then closes with a very personal prayer in verses 12–14.

Meditate on Psalm 19:12–14.

[12]Who can discern his errors? Declare me innocent from hidden faults. [13]Keep back your servant also from presumptuous sins; let them not have dominion over me! Then I shall be blameless, and innocent of great transgression. [14]Let the words of my mouth and the meditation of my heart be acceptable in your sight, O LORD, my rock and my redeemer.

Question 2: What is the connection between this prayer and verses 1–6? How might beholding God's glory in what he has created move us to confession of sin (verses 12–13) and confident trust in the Lord (verse 14)?

DAY 2—THE LORD REJOICES IN HIS WORKS

Psalm 104 begins and ends with emphatic praise to the Lord: "Bless the LORD, O my soul! O LORD my God, you are very great!" (verse 1). "Bless the LORD, O my soul! Praise the LORD!" (verse 35).

Study Psalm 104:1–9, 13, 24–27, 31–32.

[1]Bless the LORD, O my soul! O LORD my God, you are very great! You are clothed with splendor and majesty, [2]covering yourself with light as with a garment, stretching out the heavens like a

tent. [3]He lays the beams of his chambers on the waters; he makes the clouds his chariot; he rides on the wings of the wind; [4]he makes his messengers winds, his ministers a flaming fire. [5]He set the earth on its foundations, so that it should never be moved. [6]You covered it with the deep as with a garment; the waters stood above the mountains. [7]At your rebuke they fled; at the sound of your thunder they took to flight. [8]The mountains rose, the valleys sank down to the place that you appointed for them. [9]You set a boundary that they may not pass, so that they might not again cover the earth....

[13]From your lofty abode you water the mountains; the earth is satisfied with the fruit of your work....

[24] O LORD, how manifold are your works! In wisdom have you made them all; the earth is full of your creatures. [25]Here is the sea, great and wide, which teems with creatures innumerable, living things both small and great. [26]There go the ships, and Leviathan, which you formed to play in it. [27]These all look to you, to give them their food in due season....

[31]May the glory of the LORD endure forever; may the LORD rejoice in his works, [32]who looks on the earth and it trembles, who touches the mountains and they smoke!

* Question 3: Write down some of the Lord's manifold works recounted in Psalm 104. How do these works display his wisdom (verse 24)?

Question 4: In the space below, give several reasons why you think that God rejoices in his works of creation.

Day 3—Creation's Chorus of Praise

Orchestral symphonies are remarkable and beautiful because they combine a number of varied instruments—strings, winds, percussion—together in the same purpose, as each instrument plays its part in the larger piece of music. The musical unity of a symphony serves as a metaphor for the harmony of creation in praise of its Creator.

Read Psalm 148:1–14.

> ¹Praise the LORD! Praise the LORD from the heavens; praise him in the heights! ²Praise him, all his angels; praise him, all his hosts! ³Praise him, sun and moon, praise him, all you shining stars! ⁴Praise him, you highest heavens, and you waters above the heavens! ⁵Let them praise the name of the LORD! For he commanded and they were created. ⁶And he established them forever and ever; he gave a decree, and it shall not pass away. ⁷Praise the LORD from the earth, you great sea creatures and all deeps, ⁸fire and hail, snow and mist, stormy wind fulfilling his word! ⁹Mountains and all hills, fruit trees and all cedars! ¹⁰Beasts and all livestock, creeping things and flying birds! ¹¹Kings of the earth and all peoples, princes and all rulers of the earth! ¹²Young men and maidens together, old men and children! ¹³Let them praise the name of the LORD, for his name alone is exalted; his majesty is above earth and heaven. ¹⁴He has raised up a horn for his people, praise for all his saints, for the people of Israel who are near to him. Praise the LORD!

Question 5: Who or what is called upon to praise the Lord in this passage? What reasons are given for why they should praise the Lord?

* **Question 6:** The writer of Psalm 148 calls upon "great sea creatures and all deeps" to praise the Lord, even though he had
certainly never seen any of these sea creatures or been down
to the deepest parts of the sea to hear God's praise. Why
are the sea creatures and the deeps called to praise God if
human beings never hear their testimony? What reasons
can you think of for why God might be pleased with their
praise?

DAY 4—THE CREATOR IS ALSO THE REDEEMER

We saw in Romans 1:20 that creation shows forth God's *power* and his
divine *nature*. What does Isaiah 40 have to say about God's power and
nature and how they affect the lives of his people?

Meditate on Isaiah 40:25–31.

> [25]To whom then will you compare me, that I should be like him?
> says the Holy One. [26]Lift up your eyes on high and see: who
> created these? He who brings out their host by number, calling
> them all by name, by the greatness of his might, and because he is
> strong in power not one is missing. [27]Why do you say, O Jacob,
> and speak, O Israel, "My way is hidden from the LORD, and my
> right is disregarded by my God"? [28]Have you not known? Have
> you not heard? The LORD is the everlasting God, the Creator
> of the ends of the earth. He does not faint or grow weary; his
> understanding is unsearchable. [29]He gives power to the faint,
> and to him who has no might he increases strength. [30]Even

youths shall faint and be weary, and young men shall fall exhausted; [31]but they who wait for the LORD shall renew their strength; they shall mount up with wings like eagles; they shall run and not be weary; they shall walk and not faint.

* **Question 7:** In what ways is God's incomparable power illustrated in this passage? How does the Lord use his power to benefit his people?

Study Isaiah 43:1–7.

[1]But now thus says the LORD, he who created you, O Jacob, he who formed you, O Israel: "Fear not, for I have redeemed you; I have called you by name, you are mine. [2]When you pass through the waters, I will be with you; and through the rivers, they shall not overwhelm you; when you walk through fire you shall not be burned, and the flame shall not consume you. [3]For I am the LORD your God, the Holy One of Israel, your Savior. I give Egypt as your ransom, Cush and Seba in exchange for you. [4]Because you are precious in my eyes, and honored, and I love you, I give men in return for you, peoples in exchange for your life. [5]Fear not, for I am with you; I will bring your offspring from the east, and from the west I will gather you. [6]I will say to the north, Give up, and to the south, Do not withhold; bring my sons from afar and my daughters from the end of the earth, [7]everyone who is called by my name, whom I created for my glory, whom I formed and made."

Question 8: Underline all references to the Lord as Creator, and circle references to the Lord as Redeemer or Savior. What are God's people commanded to do because he is both Creator and Redeemer?

DAY 5—GOD'S DELIGHT IN HIS NEW CREATION

We have looked at a number of biblical texts which stress that God delights in his creation. But the Bible also uses creation language to describe God's work of saving and transforming his people (2 Corinthians 5:17) and making all things new (Revelation 21:5).

Consider Isaiah 65:17–25.

[17]"For behold, I create new heavens and a new earth, and the former things shall not be remembered or come into mind. [18]But be glad and rejoice forever in that which I create; for behold, I create Jerusalem to be a joy, and her people to be a gladness. [19]I will rejoice in Jerusalem and be glad in my people; no more shall be heard in it the sound of weeping and the cry of distress. [20]No more shall there be in it an infant who lives but a few days, or an old man who does not fill out his days, for the young man shall die a hundred years old, and the sinner a hundred years old shall be accursed. [21]They shall build houses and inhabit them; they shall plant vineyards and eat their fruit. [22]They shall not build and another inhabit; they shall not plant and another eat; for like the days of a tree shall the days of my people be, and my chosen shall long enjoy the work of their hands. [23]They shall not labor in vain or bear children for calamity, for they shall be the offspring

of the blessed of the LORD, and their descendants with them.
²⁴Before they call I will answer; while they are yet speaking I
will hear. ²⁵The wolf and the lamb shall graze together; the lion
shall eat straw like the ox, and dust shall be the serpent's food.
They shall not hurt or destroy in all my holy mountain," says the
LORD.

Question 9: Underline every reference to joy in this passage.
According to Isaiah 65, in what will the Lord rejoice?

Study Revelation 21:3-5.

³And I heard a loud voice from the throne saying, "Behold, the
dwelling place of God is with man. He will dwell with them, and
they will be his people, and God himself will be with them as
their God. ⁴He will wipe away every tear from their eyes, and
death shall be no more, neither shall there be mourning, nor
crying, nor pain anymore, for the former things have passed
away." ⁵And he who was seated on the throne said, "Behold, I am
making all things new." Also he said, "Write this down, for these
words are trustworthy and true."

* **Question 10:** What is the ultimate good news and the greatest
joy for God's people in the new creation?

When God makes all things new, he will make us spiritu-
ally and morally as pure as flawless crystal, he will give
us a body like the body of his glory, he will renovate all
creation to take all futility and evil and pain out of it, and
finally he himself will come to us and let us see his face.
And so forever and ever we will live with pure hearts and
glorious bodies on a new earth in the presence and the
glory of our heavenly Father.[33]

Further Up and Further In

**Read "Do You See the Joy of God in the Sun?," an online sermon at
the Desiring God website.**

Question 11: What is God's "often neglected ministry" to us?

Question 12: In what way is God's wordless communication in
the sky like a painting?

Question 13: How is the joy of God expressed in the sun?

**Read "The Pistol Star and the Power of God," an online article at
the Desiring God website.**

Question 14: What two things leave John Piper "doubly stunned" in this article?

Question 15: What is the main message of the cosmos? What response should we have to remarkable things in creation such as the Pistol Star?

-→ *While You Watch the DVD, Take Notes* ←-

Why does God rejoice in his creation?

According to Piper, why do atheists miss the joy when the sun rises?

Augustine said, "He _____ you too little who _____ anything together with you, which he _____ not for _____ _____."

How do we glorify God in our feasting?

How do we glorify God in our fasting?

—✦ *After You Watch the DVD, Discuss What You've Learned* ✦—

1. According to John Piper, God ordained that we worship him through certain means. How can physical pleasures and the beauty of creation serve as means to worship?

2. What would it look like to love good and pleasurable things in creation like chocolate, sex, and sunsets for *God's* sake? Be specific.

3. Read Psalm 27:4 together. Discuss practical ways to cultivate a single-minded joy in God in a world of competing pleasures.

—✦ *After You Discuss, Make Application* ✦—

1. What was the most meaningful part of this lesson for you? Was there a sentence, concept, or idea that really struck you? Why? Record your thoughts in the space below.

2. Plan in the next week to watch a sunrise or a sunset. Read Psalm 19:1–6 and take time for prayerful reflection. What attributes of God stand out to you as you consider that he makes the sun rise and set every day for his pleasure? Record your reflections below.

GOD'S PLEASURE IN ELECTION

A Companion Study to The Pleasures of God *DVD, Session 9*

LESSON OBJECTIVES

It is our prayer that after you have finished this lesson...
- You will embrace the biblical teaching of God's sovereign pleasure in unconditional election.
- You will praise God for setting his electing love on undeserving sinners.
- You will begin to see how the doctrine of election energizes our evangelism and prayers.

→» *Before You Watch the DVD, Study and Prepare* «←

DAY 1—WHY DID YOU BELIEVE?

Imagine two identical twins. They are both raised in the same household. They both go to church with their family. They both hear the gospel from a young age. Yet only one of the twins embraces the gospel of Jesus Christ. One day they are both killed in a car accident and they stand before God. God asks them both, "Why should I allow you into the kingdom?" The unbelieving twin has no answer, but the believing twin pleads the cross of Christ. "I have believed in your Son and his work on the cross." Then God asks the believing twin another question, "Why did you believe, and not your sibling? You both heard the same gospel; you both had the same opportunity. What made the difference between the two of you?"

> * **Question 1:** If you were that believing twin, how would you answer this question? What ultimately explains why one person believes while another does not?

In this lesson we will explore God's pleasure in election. There can be no doubt that the Bible speaks of God's choosing a people for himself. Samuel tells the people of Israel, "It has pleased the LORD to make you a people for himself" (1 Samuel 12:22). Paul writes that God "chose us in him before the foundation of the world" (Ephesians 1:4).

> **Question 2:** Define the doctrine of election in your own words. Does God choose all people or only some? On what basis does God make his choice?

The teaching of Scripture on election has been controversial. But I believe with all my heart that it is precious beyond words and a great nourishment for the Christlikeness of faith. If I understand the teaching of the Bible, God has pleasure in election. To know that this is true, and to know why it is, is to see another facet of the glory of God. And that sight has the power to make us holy and happy people.[34]

DAY 2—WHY DID GOD CHOOSE A PEOPLE FOR HIMSELF?

We begin by examining God's election of Israel in the Old Testament.

Consider Deuteronomy 7:6–8.

[6]For you are a people holy to the LORD your God. The LORD your God has chosen you to be a people for his treasured possession, out of all the peoples who are on the face of the earth. [7]It was not because you were more in number than any other people that the LORD set his love on you and chose you, for you were the fewest of all peoples, [8]but it is because the LORD loves you and is keeping the oath that he swore to your fathers, that the LORD has brought you out with a mighty hand and redeemed you from the house of slavery, from the hand of Pharaoh king of Egypt.

* **Question 3:** In light of this passage, which options below best represent God's reasons for choosing Israel and setting his love upon them? God set his love on Israel because
    a. they were more righteous than other nations.
    b. they had more faith than other nations.
    c. he loved them.
    d. they were more numerous than other nations.
    e. he was keeping his promises to Abraham, Isaac, and Jacob.

How was Israel in the Old Testament supposed to respond to the doctrine of God's election?

Study Deuteronomy 10:12–16.

[12]And now, Israel, what does the LORD your God require of you, but to fear the LORD your God, to walk in all his ways, to love him, to serve the LORD your God with all your heart and with all your soul, [13]and to keep the commandments and statutes of the LORD, which I am commanding you today for your good? [14]Behold, to the LORD your God belong heaven and the heaven of heavens, the earth with all that is in it. [15]Yet the LORD set his heart in love on your fathers and chose their offspring after them, you above all peoples, as you are this day. [16]Circumcise therefore the foreskin of your heart, and be no longer stubborn.

Question 4: According to this passage, what response did God require of his elect people? How does verse 15 relate to verse 16 in this passage?

DAY 3—JACOB I LOVED, ESAU I HATED

Not only has God chosen Israel, but the Bible also teaches that God chooses individuals. In Romans 9, Paul seeks to address the problem created by the Jewish rejection of the Messiah. God had made great promises to Israel, but their rejection of Christ makes it appear as though the Word of God has failed (Romans 9:6). Paul responds to this question of God's faithfulness by noting that "not all who are descended from Israel belong to Israel" (verse 6). He then supports this claim by noting the election of Isaac over Ishmael and Jacob over Esau.

Reflect upon Romans 9:6–13.

⁶But it is not as though the word of God has failed. For not all who are descended from Israel belong to Israel, ⁷and not all are children of Abraham because they are his offspring, but "Through Isaac shall your offspring be named." ⁸This means that it is not the children of the flesh who are the children of God, but the children of the promise are counted as offspring. ⁹For this is what the promise said: "About this time next year I will return, and Sarah shall have a son." ¹⁰And not only so, but also when Rebekah had conceived children by one man, our forefather Isaac, ¹¹though they were not yet born and had done nothing either good or bad—in order that God's purpose of election might continue, not because of works but because of him who calls— ¹²she was told, "The older will serve the younger." ¹³As it is written, "Jacob I loved, but Esau I hated."

* **Question 5:** According to Paul's teaching in this passage, why did God choose Jacob instead of Esau?

Question 6: How does God's promise (verse 9) relate to God's purpose in election (verse 11)?

What this text says is that God chooses "children of promise" (Romans 9:8) in a way that will free his choosing from human works and make it totally dependent on his own call. This is why election is called unconditional. Paul brings it out in three ways: 1) Jacob and Esau had the same parents (verse 10), unlike Isaac and Ishmael, so that parentage would not seem like the "work" that made Jacob a better candidate for election. 2) The choice was made before they were born (verse 11) so that the choice was not based on birth order. In fact God turned the tables and chose the younger. 3) The choice for Jacob was made before they had done anything good or evil. The point seems clear: election is not based on what someone does after birth. It is free and unconditional.[35]

DAY 4—THE GRACE OF GOD AND ELECTION

The book of Ephesians begins with a glorious celebration of the spiritual blessings that we have in Christ. It is an extended passage of worship and praise to the triune God who acted to save his people.

Meditate upon Ephesians 1:3–6.

[3]Blessed be the God and Father of our Lord Jesus Christ, who has blessed us in Christ with every spiritual blessing in the heavenly places, [4]even as he chose us in him before the foundation of the world, that we should be holy and blameless before him. In love [5]he predestined us for adoption as sons through Jesus Christ, according to the purpose of his will, [6]to the praise of his glorious grace, with which he has blessed us in the Beloved.

* **Question 7:** What is the first spiritual blessing that Paul praises God for? When did this spiritual blessing take place? According to verse 6, what is the ultimate purpose for God's blessing us in this way?

Predestination is one of the first gifts of the gospel, even though it preceded the death of Christ in eternity. The spotless lamb, Jesus Christ, who was slain for our sins, was foreknown before the foundation of the world (1 Pet. 1:20). Because of this, God gave us grace in Christ before the ages began (2 Tim. 1:9). Therefore, Paul says, "God predestined us for adoption through Jesus Christ" (Eph. 1:5). This predestination was God's purpose to adopt us and make us holy and blameless before him in love.... God's aim in our predestination is that we admire and make much of the glory of his grace. In other words, the aim of predestining us is that grace would be put on display as glorious, and that we would see it and savor it and sing its praises.[36]

Paul's celebration of God's grace does not end in Ephesians 1. Ephesians 2 unfolds the application of the gospel of God's glorious grace to undeserving sinners.

Consider Ephesians 2:1–9.

[1]And you were dead in the trespasses and sins [2]in which you once walked, following the course of this world, following the prince of the power of the air, the spirit that is now at work in the sons of disobedience— [3]among whom we all once lived in the passions of our flesh, carrying out the desires of the body and the mind, and were by nature children of wrath, like the rest of mankind. [4]But God, being rich in mercy, because of the great love with which he loved us, [5]even when we were dead in our trespasses, made us alive together with Christ—by grace you have been saved— [6]and raised us up with him and seated us with him in the heavenly places in Christ Jesus, [7]so that in the coming ages he might show the immeasurable riches of his grace in kindness toward us in

Christ Jesus. [8]For by grace you have been saved through faith. And this is not your own doing; it is the gift of God, [9]not a result of works, so that no one may boast.

Question 8: How does this passage describe the state of human beings prior to their salvation? In light of Paul's teaching here, how would you define the grace of God?

Day 5—Energizing Evangelism and Empowering Prayer

Does the doctrine of unconditional election make evangelism irrelevant? Why pray for the lost if God has already decided whom he will save? Some Christians reject the doctrine of unconditional election because they assume that it undermines evangelism and prayer. However, some of the most effective evangelists (such as Charles Spurgeon) and fervent pray-ers (such as George Mueller) in church history have believed strongly in God's sovereign freedom in election. Consider the following quotation from Spurgeon's autobiography:

> One week-night, when I was sitting in the house of God, I was not thinking much about the preacher's sermon, for I did not believe it. The thought struck me, "How did you come to be a Christian?" I sought the Lord. "But how did you come to seek the Lord?" The truth flashed across my mind in a moment—I should not have sought Him unless there had been some previous influence in my mind to make me seek Him. I prayed, thought I, but then I asked myself, How came I to pray? I was induced to pray by

reading the Scriptures. How came I to read the Scriptures? I did read them, but what led me to do so? Then, in a moment, I saw that God was at the bottom of it all, and that He was the Author of my faith, and so the whole doctrine of grace opened up to me, and from that doctrine I have not departed to this day, and I desire to make this my constant confession, "I ascribe my change wholly to God."[37]

Study 1 Corinthians 1:22–24.

[22]For Jews demand signs and Greeks seek wisdom, [23]but we preach Christ crucified, a stumbling block to Jews and folly to Gentiles, [24]but to those who are called, both Jews and Greeks, Christ the power of God and the wisdom of God.

Question 9: According to this passage, what makes the difference between those who reject Christ crucified and those who embrace him? How might this passage give us confidence in our evangelism?

Read Acts 18:9–11 and Colossians 4:3.

[9]And the Lord said to Paul one night in a vision, "Do not be afraid, but go on speaking and do not be silent, [10]for I am with you, and no one will attack you to harm you, for I have many in this city who are my people." [11]And he stayed a year and six months, teaching the word of God among them. (Acts 18:9–11)

³At the same time, pray also for us, that God may open to us a door for the word, to declare the mystery of Christ, on account of which I am in prison. (Colossians 4:3)

Question 10: What reasons does the Lord give Paul for why he should continue to preach the gospel in Acts 18? What does Paul want God to do in Colossians 4? How might the doctrine of election actually empower our prayers for the lost?

What I am saying is that it is not the doctrine of God's sovereignty which thwarts prayer for the conversion of sinners. On the contrary, it is the unbiblical notion of self-determination which would consistently put an end to all prayers for the lost. Prayer is a request that God do something.... Only the person who rejects human self-determination can consistently pray for God to save the lost.... In short, I do not ask God to sit back and wait for my neighbor to decide to change. I do not suggest to God that he keep his distance lest his beauty become irresistible and violate my neighbor's power of self-determination. No! I pray that he ravish my unbelieving neighbor with his beauty, that he unshackle the enslaved will, that he make the dead alive and that he suffer no resistance to stop him lest my neighbor perish.³⁸

Further Up and Further In

Read "The Pleasure of God in Election," an online sermon at the Desiring God website.

Question 11: Why does God take pleasure in election? What are God's two goals in election?

Question 12: In what ways are God's election of Israel and the church similar and different?

Question 13: What causes all three persons of the Trinity to rejoice in Luke 10:21?

Read "The Sovereignty of God and Prayer," an online article at the Desiring God website.

Question 14: How should a strong belief in God's sovereign work in conversion affect our prayers for the lost?

Question 15: In what ways does prayer function like preaching?

—➤ *While You Watch the DVD, Take Notes* ◆·—

In God's election of his people, he was acting in the overflow of his
_____. He was not constrained by anything outside
himself to _____ this people. He acted
_____. His election is _____.
How should the church respond to Israel's unbelief today?

Romans 9 shows God's freedom to do what?

What was God's purpose in free unconditional election?

What phrase in Ephesians 1 does Piper say is one of the most
important phrases in the Bible?

—➤ *After You Watch the DVD, Discuss What You've Learned* ◆·—

1. Explain in your own words why God takes pleasure in election.
   How does the doctrine of election highlight God's grace
   toward sinners?

2. What is your reaction to the teaching from this lesson? Share
    your thoughts with the group.

3. What is the relationship between God's choice of us (election)
    and our choice of God (faith)? Why is it important to reflect
    on this relationship?

—*❋ *After You Discuss, Make Application* ❋*—

1. What was the most meaningful part of this lesson for you?
    Was there a sentence, concept, or idea that really struck you?
    Why? Record your thoughts in the space below.

2. Spend a few minutes praying for a lost person whom you
    know, using the biblical truth that you have learned in this
    lesson. Write your prayer in the space below.

GOD'S PLEASURE IN BRUISING HIS SON

A Companion Study to The Pleasures of God *DVD, Session 10*

LESSON OBJECTIVES

It is our prayer that after you have finished this lesson…
- You will embrace the shocking truth that God took pleasure in bruising his Son.
- You will see the cross as a testimony to the worth and value of God above all things.
- You will marvel at the wisdom and mercy of God in planning the execution of his beloved Son.

→❋ *Before You Watch the DVD, Study and Prepare* ❋•—

DAY 1—WHO KILLED JESUS?

In Lesson 4, we saw that God's highest and deepest pleasure is in his beloved Son. He delights in his own glory as it is reflected in the face of his Son above all things. So then, what are we to make of a lesson that teaches that God took *pleasure* in the crushing and crucifixion of his Son?

To understand how this is possible, we must first ask this question: Who was responsible for the death of Jesus?

> **Question 1:** Based on your reading of Scripture, list all of the people responsible for the death of Jesus. (Hint: If you need help, read Luke 23 in your own Bible.)

John Piper tells the story of a preacher who asked an audience this question.

> I have a friend in ministry who told me of a very powerful moment in preaching. He was speaking on the Thursday night of Holy Week in a prison in Illinois. During his message on the death of Christ, he stopped and asked the inmates, "Who do you think killed Jesus?" One said, "The Jews." Another said, "The soldiers." Another said, "Pilate." Another said, "Judas." My friend said, "No, I don't think you're right." They said, "Who then?" He said, "His Father killed him."[39]

This is a shocking answer—*his Father* killed him. Can this statement be supported from the Bible?

Study Acts 4:24–28.

> [24]And when they heard it, they lifted their voices together to God and said, "Sovereign Lord, who made the heaven and the earth and the sea and everything in them, [25]who through the mouth of our father David, your servant, said by the Holy Spirit, 'Why did the Gentiles rage, and the peoples plot in vain? [26]The kings of the

earth set themselves, and the rulers were gathered together, against the Lord and against his Anointed'— [27]for truly in this city there were gathered together against your holy servant Jesus, whom you anointed, both Herod and Pontius Pilate, along with the Gentiles and the peoples of Israel, [28]to do whatever your hand and your plan had predestined to take place.

* **Question 2:** According to this passage, whose hand and whose plan stood behind the actions of Herod, Pilate, the Gentiles, and the Jews? Underline the relevant phrase. Does this fact mean that it was not evil for these men to execute the anointed of God? Explain your answer.

From all these prophecies, we know that God foresaw, and did not prevent, and therefore included in his plan that his Son would be rejected, hated, abandoned, betrayed, denied, condemned, spit upon, flogged, mocked, pierced, and killed. All these are explicitly in God's mind before they happen as things that he plans will happen to Jesus. These things did not just happen. They were foretold in God's Word. God knew they would happen and could have planned to stop them, but didn't. So they happened according to his sovereign will.

And all of them were evil. They were sin. It is sin to reject, hate, abandon, betray, deny, condemn, spit upon, flog, mock, pierce, and kill the morally perfect, infinitely worthy, divine Son of God. And yet the Bible is explicit and clear that God himself planned these things.[40]

DAY 2—GOD'S *PLEASURE* IN THE DEATH OF HIS SON?

It is one thing to say that God's hand and God's plan stood behind the Cross. It is another to say that he actually *took pleasure* in it. Is it really biblical to say that God delighted in the bruising of his Son?

> **Question 3:** Do you believe that it is biblical to say that God actually *took pleasure and delight* in bruising his beloved Son on the cross? What is your reaction to the title of this lesson?

Now examine Isaiah 53:10 and Ephesians 5:1–2.

> [10]But the LORD was pleased to crush Him, putting Him to grief; if He would render Himself as a guilt offering, He will see His offspring, He will prolong His days, and the good pleasure of the LORD will prosper in His hand. (Isaiah 53:10, NASB)

> [1]Therefore be imitators of God, as beloved children. [2]And walk in love, as Christ loved us and gave himself up for us, a fragrant offering and sacrifice to God. (Ephesians 5:1–2)

> * **Question 4:** Underline references to God's pleasure in the death of his Son. Why do you think that the execution of Jesus was a fragrant aroma to God?

Day 3—The Essence of Sin

As surprising as it may be, we can say with biblical authority that God planned (Acts 4:28) and delighted in (Isaiah 53:10) the execution of his Son. We turn now to explore *why* God was pleased when his Son was crushed. To do this, we must first understand the reason that Christ went to the cross.

Study Romans 3:23 and 1:21–23.

> [23]For all have sinned and fall short of the glory of God (Romans 3:23)

> [21]For although they knew God, they did not honor him as God or give thanks to him, but they became futile in their thinking, and their foolish hearts were darkened. [22]Claiming to be wise, they became fools, [23]and exchanged the glory of the immortal God for images resembling mortal man and birds and animals and reptiles. (Romans 1:21–23)

Question 5: From these two passages, try to give a biblical definition of sin. What is the essence of human rebellion and wickedness?

So the essence of sin is the exchanging of God's glory for lesser things. The God-belittling rebellion of human beings demands a response from God, the righteous judge. The following illustration helps us to see why this is so.

Imagine that terrorists try to assassinate the leader of your country. Their attempt fails, but many people are still killed in the attack. The terrorists are captured by the police and brought to trial. At the trial they apologize for the attack and promise not to do it again. The judge accepts their apology and decides not to punish them at all. Instead they are allowed to go free.

Question 6: What would this decision communicate to the world about the value of your leader's life and the worth of his government? What do you think should happen to this judge?

DAY 4—SHOULD GOD BE IMPEACHED?

Having examined the nature of human sin, we can now see that human rebellion creates a huge problem in the universe. But not everyone understands the nature of this problem.

Question 7: Which of the following do you think that most people in the world today consider to be the bigger problem in the universe? How do you think the Bible would address this question?
   a. The biggest problem in the universe is that God allows bad things to happen to human beings.
   b. The biggest problem in the universe is that God is treating human beings far too well.

All sin is a despising of God, before it is a damage to man. All sin is a preference for the fleeting pleasures of the world over the everlasting joy of God's fellowship.... That is the meaning of sin—failing to love God's glory above everything else. "All have sinned and fall short of the glory of God."

Therefore the problem when God passes over sin is that God seems to agree with those who despise his name and belittle his glory. He seems to be saying it is a matter of indifference that his glory is spurned. He seems to condone the low assessment of his worth.[41]

We have seen that the biggest problem in the universe is that God is passing over human sin that belittles his glory and demeans his value. In doing so, he is violating the principles of justice.

Read Genesis 18:25; 2 Chronicles 19:7; Job 8:3; Proverbs 17:15; and Romans 9:14.

[25]Far be it from you to do such a thing, to put the righteous to death with the wicked, so that the righteous fare as the wicked! Far be that from you! Shall not the Judge of all the earth do what is just? (Genesis 18:25)

[7]Now then, let the fear of the LORD be upon you. Be careful what you do, for there is no injustice with the LORD our God, or partiality or taking bribes. (2 Chronicles 19:7)

[3]Does God pervert justice? Or does the Almighty pervert the right? (Job 8:3)

[15]He who justifies the wicked and he who condemns the righteous are both alike an abomination to the LORD. (Proverbs 17:15)

¹⁴What shall we say then? Is there injustice on God's part? By no means! (Romans 9:14)

* **Question 8:** What do these verses tell us about the necessity of God's justice when it comes to judging sin and wrongdoing?

Justice proceeds on the principle laid down in Proverbs 17:15, "He who justifies the wicked and he who condemns the righteous are both alike—an abomination to the LORD." We impeach judges who acquit the guilty. Our moral sensibility is outraged when wrong is given legal sanction. Yet at the heart of the Christian gospel stands the sentence: God justifies the ungodly (Romans 4:5). He acquits the guilty. That is the gospel. But how can it be right for God to do that?⁴²

DAY 5—CHRIST VINDICATES GOD AND JUSTIFIES SINNERS

Piper has called Romans 3:23–26 the most important paragraph in the Bible because it addresses the crucial question of how a righteous God could justify or declare righteous sinners.

Reflect upon Romans 3:23–26.

²³For all have sinned and fall short of the glory of God, ²⁴and are justified by his grace as a gift, through the redemption that is in Christ Jesus, ²⁵whom God put forward as a propitiation by his blood, to be received by faith. This was to show God's righteous-

ness, because in his divine forbearance he had passed over former sins. ²⁶It was to show his righteousness at the present time, so that he might be just and the justifier of the one who has faith in Jesus.

* **Question 9:** How does this passage solve the problem created by God's passing over of sins committed by rebels? How is God able to maintain his righteousness and have mercy on people?

What was in Jesus' mind as he prepared to die on the cross as the righteous for the unrighteous? According to the gospel of John, Jesus was supremely concerned with glorifying his Father.

Study John 12:27–28; 13:31; and 17:4.

²⁷Now is my soul troubled. And what shall I say? "Father, save me from this hour"? But for this purpose I have come to this hour. ²⁸Father, glorify your name." Then a voice came from heaven: "I have glorified it, and I will glorify it again." (John 12:27–28)

³¹When he had gone out, Jesus said, "Now is the Son of Man glorified, and God is glorified in him." (John 13:31)

⁴I glorified you on earth, having accomplished the work that you gave me to do. (John 17:4)

Question 10: How did the death of Jesus on the cross magnify the worth of God's glory?

All of Jesus' work was designed to honor the worth of his
Father's glory. Everything Jesus suffered, he suffered for
the sake of God's glory. Therefore, all his pain and shame
and humiliation and dishonor served to magnify the Father's glory, because they showed how infinitely valuable
God's glory is, that such a loss should be suffered to demonstrate its worth. When we look at the wracking pain
and death of the perfectly innocent and infinitely worthy
Son of God on the cross, and hear that he endured it all
so that the glory of his Father, desecrated by sinners,
might be restored, then we know that God has *not* denied
the value of his own glory; he has *not* been untrue to
himself; he has *not* ceased to uphold his honor and display his glory; he is just—*and* the justifier of the ungodly.[43]

FURTHER UP AND FURTHER IN

**Read "The Pleasure of God in Bruising the Son," an online sermon
at the Desiring God website.**

Question 11: What troubling reality has emerged from our study
of the pleasures of God?

Question 12: How does John Piper demonstrate that we should
translate Isaiah 53:10 as "The LORD *was pleased* to bruise him"?

Question 13: From this sermon, give two reasons why the Father
took pleasure in the bruising of his Son.

Read "Did Christ Die for Us or for God?," an online sermon at the Desiring God website.

> **Question 14:** Summarize in your own words the differences between a secular mind-set and a biblical mind-set. According to each mind-set, what is the biggest problem in the universe?

> **Question 15:** How does Piper answer the question, "How can it be loving for God to be so self-exalting in the work of the cross?"

—❖ *While You Watch the DVD, Take Notes* ❖—

You need to know yourself loved with a kind of love not ultimately dependent on _____ but on _____.
The doctrine of election assures us of success in what?

If sinners are to be elect and saved, God's _____ must be upheld, and his _____ must be vindicated.
According to Piper, what is the most important paragraph in the Bible?

What is the solution to the problem of God's righteousness in saving sinners?

→❖ *After You Watch the DVD, Discuss What You've Learned* ❖←

1. Why should the doctrine of election bring security to the believer?

2. Discuss the "huge" problem in the universe, as set forth in this lesson. How often do you feel the gravity of this problem?

3. What new aspects of the glory of God have you seen in reflecting upon the pleasure of God in bruising his Son?

→❖ *After You Discuss, Make Application* ❖←

1. What was the most meaningful part of this lesson for you? Was there a sentence, concept, or idea that really struck you? Why? Record your thoughts in the space below.

2. In the space below, write out an explanation of the Cross of Christ from a human-centered perspective. Then write out an explanation of the Cross from a God-centered perspective. Spend some time praying that God would continue to awaken you to *his glory* in the Cross.

REVIEW AND CONCLUSION

LESSON OBJECTIVES

It is our prayer that after you have finished this lesson...
- You will be able to summarize and synthesize what you've learned.
- You will hear what others in your group have learned.
- You will share with others how you have begun to see God in a new light.

WHAT HAVE YOU LEARNED?

There are no study questions to answer in preparation for this lesson. Instead, spend your time writing a few paragraphs that explain what you've learned in this group study. To help you do this, you may choose to review the notes you've taken in the previous lessons. Then, after you've written down what you've learned, write down some questions that you still have about anything addressed in these lessons. Be prepared to share these reflections and questions with the group in the next lesson.

NOTES

Use this space to record anything in the group discussion that you want to remember.

LEADERS GUIDE

As the leader of this group study, **it is imperative that you are completely familiar with this study guide** and *The Pleasures of God* DVD set. Therefore, it is our strong recommendation that you (1) read and understand the introduction, (2) skim each lesson, surveying its layout and content, and (3) read the entire Leaders Guide *before* you begin the group study and distribute the study guides.

BEFORE LESSON 1

Before the first lesson, you will need to know approximately how many participants you will have in your group study. **Each participant will need his or her own study guide!** Therefore, be sure to order enough study guides. You will distribute these study guides at the beginning of the first lesson.

It is also our strong recommendation that you, as the leader, familiarize yourself with this study guide and *The Pleasures of God* DVD set in order to answer any questions that might arise and also to ensure that each group session runs smoothly and maximizes the learning of the participants. It is not necessary for you to preview *The Pleasures of God* in its entirety—although it certainly wouldn't hurt!—but you should be prepared to navigate your way through each DVD menu.

DURING LESSON 1

Each lesson is designed for a one-hour group session. Lessons 2–12 require preparatory work from the participants before this group session. Lesson 1, however, requires no preparation on the part of the participants.

The following schedule is how we suggest that you use the first hour of your group study:

Introduction to the Study Guide (10 minutes)

Introduce this study guide and *The Pleasures of God* DVD. Share with the group why you chose to lead the group study using these resources. Inform your group of the commitment that this study will require and motivate them to work hard. Pray for the twelve-week study and ask God for the grace you will need. Then distribute one study guide to each participant. You may read the introduction aloud, if you want, or you may immediately turn the group to Lesson 1.

Personal Introductions (15 minutes)

Since group discussion will be an integral part of this guided study, it is crucial that each participant feels welcome and safe. The goal of each lesson is for every participant to contribute to the discussion in some way. Therefore, during these 15 minutes have the participants introduce themselves. You may choose to use the questions listed in the section titled "About Yourself," or you may ask questions of your own choosing.

Discussion (25 minutes)

Transition from the time of introductions to the discussion questions, listed under the heading "A Preview of *The Pleasures of God*." Invite everyone in the class to respond to these questions, but don't let the discussion become too involved. These questions are designed to spark interest and generate questions. The aim is not to come to definitive answers yet.

Review and Closing (10 minutes)

End the group session by reviewing Lesson 2 with the group participants and informing them of the preparation that they must do before the group meets again. Encourage them to be faithful in preparing for the next lesson. Answer any questions that the group may have and then close in prayer.

BEFORE LESSONS 2-11

As the group leader, you should do all the preparation for each lesson that is required of the group participants, that is, the ten study questions. Furthermore, it is highly recommended that you complete the entire

"Further Up and Further In" section. This is not required of the group participants, but it will enrich your preparation and help you to guide and shape the conversation more effectively.

The group leader should also preview the session of *The Pleasures of God* that will be covered in the next lesson. So, for example, if the group participants are doing the preparatory work for Lesson 3, you should preview *The Pleasures of God,* Session 2 before the group meets and views it. Previewing each session will better equip you to understand the material and answer questions. If you want to pause the DVD in the midst of the session in order to clarify or discuss, previewing the session will allow you to plan where you want to take your pauses.

Finally, you may want to supplement or modify the discussion questions or the application assignment. Please remember that **this study guide is a resource**; any additions or changes you make that better match the study to your particular group are encouraged. This study guide should function as a helpful tool and *resource.* As the group leader, your own discernment, creativity, and guidance are invaluable, and you should adapt the material as you see fit.

**Plan for about two hours of your own preparation
before each lesson!**

DURING LESSONS 2–11

Again, let us stress that during Lessons 2–11 you may use the group time in whatever way you desire. The following schedule, however, is what we suggest:

Discussion (10 minutes)

Begin your time with prayer. The tone you set in your prayer will likely be impressed upon the group participants. If your prayer is serious and heartfelt, the group participants will be serious about prayer; if your prayer is hasty, sloppy, or a token gesture, the group participants will share this same attitude toward prayer. So model the kind of praying that you desire your group to imitate. Remember, the blood of Jesus has bought your access to the throne of grace.

After praying, review the preparatory work that the participants completed. How did they answer the questions? Which questions did they find to be the most interesting or the most confusing? What observations or insights can they share with the group? If you would like to review some tips for leading productive discussions, please turn to the appendix at the end of this Leaders Guide.

The group participants will be provided an opportunity to apply what they've learned in Lessons 2–11. As the group leader, you can choose whether it would be appropriate for the group to discuss these assignments during this ten-minute time slot.

DVD Viewing (30 minutes)

Play the session from *The Pleasures of God* DVD set that corresponds to the lesson you're studying. You may choose to pause the DVD at crucial points to check for understanding and provide clarification. Or you may choose to watch the DVD without interruption.[44]

Discussion and Closing (20 minutes)

Foster discussion on what was taught during John Piper's session. You may do this by first reviewing the DVD notes (under the heading "While You Watch the DVD, Take Notes") and then proceeding to the discussion questions, listed under the heading "After You Watch the DVD, Discuss What You've Learned." These discussion questions are meant to be springboards that launch the group into further and deeper discussion. Don't feel confined to these questions if the group discussion begins to move in other helpful directions.

Close the time by briefly reviewing the application section and the homework that is expected for the next lesson. Pray and dismiss.

BEFORE LESSON 12

It is important that you encourage the group participants to complete the preparatory work for Lesson 12. This assignment invites participants to reflect on what they've learned and what remaining questions they still have. As the group leader, this would be a helpful assignment for you to complete as well. In addition, you may want to write down the key concepts of this DVD series that you want the group participants to walk away with.

DURING LESSON 12

The group participants are expected to complete a reflection exercise as part of their preparation for Lesson 12. The bulk of the group time during this last lesson should be focused on reviewing and synthesizing what was learned. Encourage all participants to share some of their recorded thoughts. Attempt to answer any remaining questions that they might have.

To close this last lesson, you might want to spend extended time in prayer. If appropriate, take prayer requests relating to what the participants have learned in these twelve weeks, and bring these requests to God.

It would be completely appropriate for you, the group leader, to give a final charge or word of exhortation to end this group study. Speak from your heart and out of the overflow of the joy that you have in God.

Please receive our blessing for all of you group leaders who choose to use this study guide:

> *The LORD bless you and keep you; the LORD make his*
> *face to shine upon you and be gracious to you; the LORD*
> *lift up his countenance upon you and give you peace.*
> *(Numbers 6:24–26)*

APPENDIX A: SIX-SESSION INTENSIVE OPTION

We understand that there are circumstances which may prohibit a group from devoting twelve sessions to this study. In view of this, we have designed a six-session intensive option for groups that need to complete the material in less time. In the intensive option, the group should meet for two hours each week. Here is our suggestion for how to complete the material in six weeks:

Week 1   Introduction to the Study Guide and Lesson 1
Week 2   Lessons 2 and 3 (DVD Sessions 1 and 2)
Week 3   Lessons 4 and 5 (DVD Sessions 3 and 4)
Week 4   Lessons 6 and 7 (DVD Sessions 5 and 6)
Week 5   Lessons 8 and 9 (DVD Sessions 7 and 8)
Week 6   Lessons 10 and 11 (DVD Sessions 9 and 10)

Notice that we have not included Lesson 12 in the intensive option. Moreover, because each participant is required to complete two lessons per week, it will be necessary to combine the number of "days" within each lesson so that all of the material is covered. Thus, for example, during Week 2 in the intensive option, each participant will complete

- Lesson 2, Days 1 and 2, on the first day
- Lesson 2, Days 3 and 4, on the second day
- Lesson 2, Day 5 and Lesson 3, Day 1, on the third day
- Lesson 3, Days 2 and 3, on the fourth day
- Lesson 3, Days 4 and 5, on the fifth day

Because of the amount of material, we recommend that participants focus on questions marked with an asterisk (*) first and then, if time permits, complete the rest of the questions.

APPENDIX B: LEADING PRODUCTIVE DISCUSSIONS

Note: This material has been adapted from curricula produced by Bethlehem College and Seminary, a ministry of Bethlehem Baptist Church. It is used by permission.

I t is our conviction that the best group leaders foster an environment in their groups which engages the participants. Most people learn by solving problems or by working through things that provoke curiosity or concern. Therefore, we discourage you from ever lecturing for the entire lesson. Although a group leader will constantly shape conversation, clarifying and correcting as needed, he or she will probably not talk for the majority of the lesson. This study guide is meant to facilitate an investigation into biblical truth—an investigation that is shared by the group leader and the participants. Therefore, we encourage you to adopt the posture of a fellow learner who invites participation from everyone in the group.

It might surprise you how eager people can be to share what they have learned in preparing for each lesson. Therefore, you should invite participation by asking your group participants to share their discoveries. Here are some of our tips on facilitating discussion that is engaging and helpful:

- Don't be uncomfortable with silence initially. Once the first participant shares his or her response, others will be likely to join in. But if you cut the silence short by prompting them, then they are more likely to wait for you to prompt them every time.

- Affirm every answer, if possible, and draw out the participants by asking for clarification. Your aim is to make them feel comfortable sharing their ideas and learning, so be extremely hesitant to shut down a group member's contribution or trump it with your own. This does not mean, however, that you shouldn't correct false ideas—just do it in a spirit of gentleness and love.

- Don't allow a single person or group of persons to dominate the discussion. Involve everyone, if possible, and intentionally invite participation from those who are more reserved or hesitant.

- Labor to show the significance of their study. Emphasize the things that the participants could not have learned without doing the homework.

- Avoid talking too much. The group leader should not monopolize the discussion, but rather guide and shape it. If the group leader does the majority of the talking, the participants will be less likely to interact and engage, and therefore they will not learn as much. Avoid constantly adding the definitive last word.

- The group leader should feel the freedom to linger on a topic or question if the group demonstrates interest. The group leader should also pursue digressions that are helpful and relevant. There is a balance to this, however. The group leader *should* attempt to cover the material. So avoid the extreme of constantly wandering off topic, but also avoid the extreme of limiting the conversation in a way that squelches curiosity or learning.

- The group leader's passion, or lack of it, is infectious. Therefore, if you demonstrate little enthusiasm for the material, it is almost inevitable that your participants will likewise be bored. But if you have a genuine excitement for what you are studying, and if you truly think Bible study is worthwhile, then your group will be impacted positively. Therefore, it is our recommendation that before you come to the group, you spend enough time working through the homework and praying, so that you can overflow with genuine enthusiasm for the Bible and for God in your group. This point cannot be stressed enough. Delight yourself in God and in his Word!

NOTES

1. John Piper, *The Pleasures of God* (Colorado Springs, CO: Multnomah, 2012), 7.
2. While this study guide is ideally suited for a twelve-session study, it is possible to complete it in six sessions. For instructions on how to use this study guide for a six-session group study, turn to Appendix A: "Six-Session Intensive Option."
3. Although this resource is designed to be used in a group setting, it can also be used by independent learners. Such learners would have to decide for themselves how to use this resource in the most beneficial way. We would suggest doing everything but the group discussion, if possible.
4. Thirty minutes is only an approximation. Some sessions are longer; others are shorter.
5. Questions marked with an asterisk (*) are questions that we deem to be particularly significant. If your group is completing this study using the six-session intensive option, we recommend that you complete these questions first and then, if time permits, complete the remaining questions. For more information, see Appendix A, "Six-Session Intensive Option."
6. John Piper, "Your Love Is Better Than Life," an online sermon at the Desiring God website.
7. Henry Scougal, *The Life of God in the Soul of Man,* quoted in Piper, *The Pleasures of God,* 4.
8. John Piper, "What Is Christian Hedonism?," an online article at the Desiring God website.
9. Piper, *The Pleasures of God,* 12–13.
10. John Piper, "How to Drink Orange Juice to the Glory of God," an online article at the Desiring God website.

11. John Piper, "The Pleasure of God in His Son," an online sermon at the Desiring God website.

12. Henry Scougal, *The Life of God in the Soul of Man* (Ross-shire, Scotland: Christian Focus, 2001), 68.

13. Scougal, *The Life of God in the Soul of Man,* 53.

14. Piper, *The Pleasures of God,* 34.

15. Piper, *The Pleasures of God,* 13.

16. Piper, *The Pleasures of God,* 15.

17. Piper, *The Pleasures of God,* 70.

18. Jonathan Edwards, quoted in Piper, *The Pleasures of God,* 71.

19. John Piper, "The Pleasure of God in His Name," an online sermon at the Desiring God website.

20. Westminster Confession of Faith, sec. 3.1.

21. Piper, *The Pleasures of God,* 38.

22. John Piper, "Risk and the Cause of God," an online sermon at the Desiring God website.

23. Piper, *The Pleasures of God,* 46.

24. Patrick Johnstone, quoted in Piper, *The Pleasures of God,* 49–50.

25. John Piper, "The Sale of Joseph and the Son of God," an online sermon at the Desiring God website.

26. John Piper, "Job: Reverent in Suffering," an online sermon at the Desiring God website.

27. John Piper, "Are There Two Wills in God?," an online article at the Desiring God website.

28. John Piper, "The Hardening of Pharaoh and the Hope of the World," an online sermon at the Desiring God website.

29. Piper, *The Pleasures of God,* 66.

30. John Piper, "Displays of God Remove the Excuse for Failed Worship," online sermon at the Desiring God website.

31. C. S. Lewis, *Mere Christianity,* in *A Mind Awake: An Anthology of C. S. Lewis,* ed. Clyde Kilby (New York: Harcourt, Brace and World, 1968), 210–211.

32. Piper, *The Pleasures of God,* 69.

33. John Piper, "Behold, I Make All Things New," an online sermon at the Desiring God website.
34. Piper, *The Pleasures of God,* 106.
35. Piper, *The Pleasures of God,* 115.
36. John Piper, *God Is the Gospel* (Wheaton, IL: Crossway, 2005), 118.
37. Charles Spurgeon, quoted in John Piper, "What We Believe About the Five Points of Calvinism," an online article at the Desiring God website.
38. John Piper, "The Sovereignty of God and Prayer," an online sermon at the Desiring God website.
39. Piper, *The Pleasures of God,* 144–45.
40. John Piper, "Judas Iscariot, the Suicide of Satan, and the Salvation of the World," an online sermon at the Desiring God website.
41. John Piper, "Did Christ Die for Us or for God?," an online sermon at the Desiring God website.
42. Piper, *The Pleasures of God,* 146–47.
43. Piper, *The Pleasures of God,* 149–50.
44. Thirty minutes is only an approximation. Some of the sessions are shorter while some are longer. You may need to budget your group time differently, depending upon which session you are viewing.